MW01235024

Wherein the Lilies Grow

Wherein the Lilies Grow

Jo Crosby

AMBASSADOR INTERNATIONAL
GREENVILLE, SOUTH CAROLINA & BELFAST, NORTHERN IRELAND

www.ambassador-international.com

Wherein the Lilies Grow

© 2012 by Jo Crosby
All rights reserved

Printed in the United States of America

ISBN: 978-1-62020-017-9
eISBN: 978-1-62020-018-6

Cover Design and Page Layout by Matthew Mulder

Unless otherwise noted, all Scripture quotations taken from THE HOLY BIBLE, NEW INTERNATIONAL VERSION®, NIV® Copyright © 1973, 1978, 1984, 2011 by Biblica, Inc.™ Used by permission. All rights reserved worldwide.

Scripture quotations marked (NLT) are taken from the Holy Bible, New Living Translation, copyright © 1996, 2004, 2007 by Tyndale House Foundation. Used by permission of Tyndale House Publishers, Inc., Carol Stream, Illinois 60188. All rights reserved.

Scripture taken from The Message. Copyright © 1993, 1994, 1995, 1996, 2000, 2001, 2002. Used by permission of NavPress Publishing Group.

AMBASSADOR INTERNATIONAL
Emerald House
427 Wade Hampton Blvd.
Greenville, SC 29609, USA
www.ambassador-international.com

AMBASSADOR BOOKS
The Mount
2 Woodstock Link
Belfast, BT6 8DD, Northern Ireland, UK
www.ambassador-international.com

The colophon is a trademark of Ambassador

For John

—for believing and abiding with me in the shade of God's favorite tree

Endorsements

I have known Jo Crosby for 15 years as a friend, and we have worked together as Christian counselors for 10. We often hear the phrase, "she is a woman after God's own heart". This is evident in Jo Crosby through her actions, her Christian counsel, but most importantly her heart. Many years ago Jo shared one of her dreams was to write a book that would give others a deeper understanding of God's love and compassion for us. God has answered this dream in an amazing way through her book Wherein the Lilies Grow. Read this book, it will impact your life in an astounding way.

Keith Niager, MSW, LCSW, The Barnabas Center for Counseling, Savannah, Georgia

Jo Crosby has walked some difficult roads in life that many of us will never have to travel. As the Lord has led her, He has blessed her with the strength to endure and the words to share her journey of deepening faith and trust in Him. What an encouragement to me those words have been!

Elizabeth Harrelson, Trauma survivor by the grace of God

Jo is an energetic, positive force for God in the Savannah area. Jo is active within our community, respected by her peers in the Family Counseling arena, and beloved by the women she has led in bible study for years. As a lay person, serving alongside Jo as a member of the Savannah Christian (local church), I heartily endorse Jo's interactive writing style, her Spirit-led approach to hurting people, and her aggressive approach to problem-solving and family communication issues!

Jody Blazer, Bible Study Colleague

Jo Crosby so well expresses what I wish I could say. She describes the majesty of God's creation beautifully and poetically, putting into words the reactions I sometimes have, but can find no words to communicate. Her keen observations of nature, the God who made it, and the lessons He would have us learn are refreshing breezes to all of us, and especially to those who are so earth bound that they have missed God's sheer beauty.

Dr. Eleanor A. Daniel, Dorothy Keister Walker Professor of Christian Education Emeritus, Emmanuel school of Religion, Johnson City, TN.

I have been truly blessed by Jo Crosby. Her insightful writings and teachings were an inspiration to me at a very difficult time in my life. She helped me to understand that in times of strife we have to rely on Jesus. Don't miss the opportunity to be blessed by this book.

Dr. Mikki Garcia, Executive Director, Exceptional Children/K-8/Middle Schools, Savannah, Georgia

Absolutely beautiful! Jo's reflections on the beauty of God's creations and the way they reflect God's intimate relationship with us would melt the hardest heart. Her words bring softness, understanding, compassion, profound faith, and a bit of light hearted humor to the fortunate reader. Her book will not be relegated to the bookshelf, but will remain on the nightstand to be read and re-read for inspiration and enjoyment.

Jane Adams Nangle, Mother, Lawyer, & Mental Health Advocate

In the darkest nights of my soul, Jo Crosby's words have come straight from our Father to rest gently on my heart. These heavenly inspirations have been a beautiful encouragement for me through my own battle with breast cancer. Her gentle, kind, and courageous spirit is celebrated in the movement of her words across each page, as Jesus offers life through Jo with each word so carefully and tenderly placed.

Barbara Feemster, Breast Cancer Survivor

Jo's writings have helped me to understand God's love in a deeper more personal way. She has the ability to take words and give them life.

Maggie Gignilliat, RN, MSW

Jo Crosby has the uncanny ability to communicate with women, no matter what the level of their spiritual maturity. They can feel the presence of Jesus when she speaks and it is His wisdom she imparts. God gets the glory for whatever she writes, speaks, or lives.

Joy Gill, Fellow Sojourner & Warrior for Christ

Contents

Everyday Gardening

In my everyday walk,
Tending flowers and praying are concomitant.
My garden is as much about my following
As it is about the seeds I plant.
Among the flowers, my heart can hear God talk,
And my eyes can see His creation sing.

*"How great is the love the Father has lavished on us, that we should be
called children of God! And that is what we are!"*

—1 John 3:1

Preface

"Poetry is the spontaneous outflow of powerful feelings: it takes its origins from emotion recollected in tranquility."

—William Wordsworth

HAVING DOODLED WITH WORDS SINCE I could write, I am not surprised that poetry showed up in the pages of my journal. Drawn to both the rhythmical and personal nature of this form of expression, I found myself writing poetry to communicate a wide range of feelings and thoughts. Perhaps it was not my initial intent to write a book of poetry; however, it was *always* my desire to tell a story, and as I have often discovered, following God requires me to check my personal intentions at the door. In a journal, my feelings and thoughts often loom larger than life as pages are filled with words. Writing poetry gives my pen a tighter boundary while challenging me to keep the depth of emotion uncompromised.

The origins of this story began some time ago, when I started walking through both garden beauty and what I refer to as a time in the wasteland. This time was characterized by both difficulty and blessings. As my feet sank into garden soil and my face pressed into the putrid smell of wilderness dirt, I claimed the promises that are true and available to God's children. The whimsical nature of poetry provided a venue for me to write about circumstances in the wasteland that did not always make sense—circumstances that broke my heart. The beauty of the garden served to remind me that when life whirled in a seemingly uncontrollable pattern, God was in perfect control.

As a counselor, I had taught others that difficult circumstances create chaos, and chaos is noisy—noisy emotionally and noisy physically. In the wasteland, my life became *chaotically noisy*. I longed for a quiet place. I longed for rest. I longed for beauty. But mostly, I longed to be close to the Lord, and thankfully He longed to be close to me!

I remember the moment the words *day lily garden* fell upon my ears and into my heart. Standing on the back porch with my sister, I listened as she discussed a recent trip to the day lily garden. I noticed that as my sister talked, she glowed. Her recollection of colors and blooms fascinated my imagination. I left her home knowing that she had stumbled across something spectacular, and I wanted to be a part of it. Captivated by her enthusiasm, I accepted her invitation to dig lilies one afternoon, and the rest is history—a history that would show me smitten by the deep, rich beauty of these flowers.

I may have ventured to the day lily garden behind my sister's feet, but God was clearly walking before me. In addition to providing beauty, the day lily garden became my beloved place of quiet rest with God. Walking among the velvety blooms, not only did I see myself reflected, but I also found the time to be still, to listen, and to genuinely converse with Him. Among the lilies, the Spirit of God ministered to my heart through scripture. Over the petals and into the dirt, I poured a wealth of emotions, and when I had no words, God gave me permission to be quiet. Just as God rebuked and halted the wind that blew across the Sea of Galilee, so it was in my life. The resting peace I found in the day lily garden was protected from the chaotic noise that blew elsewhere in my life. Extremes of both tears and laughter have fallen from my heart over the petals I love, their beauty never failing to pull the worship from my heart.

As worship changed my heart, true healing followed. As I abided in Christ, I found strength and courage. In the stench of the wasteland, my feet learned to skip and dance. While words could never fully express the process or the intimate manner in which God worked in my life, the garden became my place of communicating with Him, and writing poetry became my way of dancing with the words.

As I like to start my day, so I have started each chapter in this book—with focused devotion. The entries are taken from my personal journal. Some of them were written for teaching purposes, while others were penned for personal reflection. Some of them were written in my head as I sat receiving chemotherapy, and others were written as I sat beside the wrestling mat watching my son engage in the sport he loves.

Storytellers often begin their tales with poetry, and writers have long sought to capture the essence of love through the power of words. God, both a storyteller and a writer, penned a story of love on my heart. The poems in this book are expressions of my time with Him—my *Abba Father* and the true *Gardener*. They are intended to reflect His heart and thereby shape the hearts of those who read them. He is always surprising me with the tiniest details of creation and blessing me with snapshots of His splendor; therefore, they are individually linked to His Word. Even as I read back through my writing, I can see God revealing pictures of His splendor—of Himself—to me.

It was momentarily tempting to share only the positive upside of my journey; however, I feared that approach would negate, normalize, or diminish the magnitude of God's blessing, His love, and His provision. My prayer is that through the ordinary moments of my story, God will be seen as *divinely* extraordinary. He planted a garden for me; He never left my side in the wasteland; and I am beholden to

Him. It is with joy and devotion to God, *my Gardener*, that I share these doodled words.

Blessings,
Jo

God is
Sheer Beauty

Sunsets and Lizards

OFTEN, I SEEK AND FIND God in the majestic. The beauty of a breathtaking sunset or the twisty nature of a timeworn tree can quickly move me to acknowledging His power and presence in my life. One ordinary day, He taught me a lesson and answered a prayer using a lizard and a broom.

I was sitting in my kitchen having lunch, when a small movement on the windowsill caught my eye. I had an instant stomach pang because I knew, without fully looking, what creatures make those types of movements—small green lizards. A confirming look stole my appetite. I would have been no less upset to discover a crocodile sunning in my backyard. Now, that may be irrational thinking to you, but I am quite afraid of lizards. I have never liked them! They jump and they're very fast. The thought of one crawling unhindered throughout my house is almost nauseating.

Therefore, I had a dilemma: How do I get this lizard out

19

of my house? As I mentally scrolled through various options, something strange happened. I really looked at the lizard. He was *beautiful*. He could not have been more than three inches long, and his features were very delicate. His skin was perfect, and the brilliant shade of green reflecting off his skin changed to an odd grey when his foot touched the window lock. He was really amazing. I knew that only God could make something so beautiful and so perfect. The same God that supplies my daily needs supplies his. Well, now I had a new dilemma: I needed to get him out of my house, but killing him wasn't an option.

My first plan to capture him in a plastic butter tub failed quickly when he made a jump toward me. He may have been beautiful, but I still didn't want him touching me. So, I moved to plan "B": *the broom*.

Lizards apparently do not like brooms, because he ran on the first sight of it. What happened next is not so pretty; I will spare you the play by play, but let's just say that the more I tried to persuade him to ride the broom to safety, the more he and I both panicked.

The events that transpired next are just a "God thing." This lizard turned on the windowsill, lay down, and made eye contact with me. It was really an odd moment. But, God very clearly and carefully used those minutes to answer a prayer in my life.

Teary-eyed, I grasped the lesson and acknowledged that God was addressing the thoughts of my heart. With the lizard still staring at me, I replaced the broom on the windowsill. He carefully turned and slowly walked onto the straw-lined edge. This lizard was cooperating with plan "C"—being *carried*, and he stood motionless as I transported him from inside my house to outside. As he disembarked beside my front door, I watched him scamper toward the border grass and wondered if he knew that the Creator had needed him for a teaching illustration.

My lizard story is affirmation that God is always at work in my life. He does not miss one tear that falls from my cheek, and He is faithful to answer my prayer. He sees my day; He sees my face, as David wrote in Psalm 56:8: "Record my lament; list my tears on your scroll—are they not in your record?"

I am thankful for the Living God who loves me enough to creatively span the distance between a breathtaking sunset and the end of my broom. If I had not learned through the study of scripture to look for the power and presence of God in the ordinary as well as the majestic, I might have missed my lizard lesson. I might have missed the wonder of God at work in my ordinary day.

From a lawn filled with the greening grass of spring to the dancing tendrils of a curly willow's frame to the silly antics of my cat, I see the divine hand of my Father at work in His creation, and it captivates my heart. The very hands that were pierced at Calvary drip the summer blueberries with sweetness and make the time to catch tears. *God is sheer beauty.* The psalmist writes:

"On your feet now—applaud God! Bring a gift of laughter, sing yourselves into his presence. Know this: God is God, and God, God. He made us; we didn't make him. We're his people, his well-tended sheep. Enter with the password: 'Thank you!' Make yourselves at home, talking praise. Thank him. Worship him. For God is sheer beauty, all-generous in love, loyal always and ever.

—Psalm 100 (The Message)

Look and See

Early, by morning's first light, the lilies are kissed.
I stand staring at the petals of deep burgundy,
And I marvel at the creative wonder of God,
Who would take the time to paint such beauty
For us, who are simply willing to look, to see.
This art from His hand could have been so easily missed.

"For the Lord is the great God, the great King above all gods. In his hand are the depths of the earth, and the mountain peaks belong to him. The sea is his, for he made it, and his hands formed the dry land. Come, let us bow down in worship, let us kneel before the Lord our Maker; for he is our God and we are the people of his pasture, the flock under his care."

—Psalm 95:3–7

Bed of Grass

Grass, tall and green,
covering a small area in the garden,
creating a soft, pillowed patch,
perfect for an afternoon nap
or a hiding place for remaining unseen;
Grass, tall and green
spreads underneath my frame,
watching my stress level meet its match,
buffering the exclamation of my name,
swaying; thereby shading my face,
Green grass, tall like an armament,
providing a place
wherein my afternoon was spent.

*"May the God of hope fill you with all joy and peace as you trust in him,
so that you may overflow with hope by the power of the Holy Spirit."*

—Romans 15:13

Curly Willow

The curly willow's winding arms,
Begging me to swing with them in the wind,
Creating a dance of slow, graceful movements,
Reaching for my hair, tickling my nose as they pass,
Beguiling me with their tortellini-like charms.

"I will praise you, O Lord, with all my heart; before the 'gods' I will sing your praise. I will bow down toward your holy temple and will praise your name for your love and faithfulness, for you have exalted above all things your name and your word. When I called, you answered me; you made me bold and stouthearted."

—Psalm 138:1–3

Rose Relationship

This wandering, sprawling rose takes her place,
And much more than her fair share of the bed.
Her stingy nature I find I can easily forgive,
When blooms delicately detailed as fine lace
Grow on vines that extend over my head.
Her unquestionable beauty I was admiring this morning,
When teasingly I gave her this warning,
"You can consume the nutrients in the soil and the space
As long as you let the lilies growing nearby live!"
She shrugged me off by way of thorns,
Sticking into our relationship like words left unsaid.
Beauty has secured her place in my garden,
And, she knows I am smitten by the area she adorns.

"For since the creation of the world God's invisible qualities—his eternal
power and divine nature—have been clearly seen, being understood from
what has been made, so that men are without excuse."

—Romans 1:20

Callie Cat

A snail peeked at me;
I was moving the leaf that provided his shade.
As I upset his quiet place,
I caught a quick glimpse of his face,
Surprising me—Surprising him!
With little thought, I scooped him in my spade
And launched him into my cat's grin!
Oops!

"Now the Lord God had planted a garden in the east, in Eden; and there he put the man he had formed."

—Genesis 2:8

Leaving Beauty

Dogwoods, pines, azaleas,
hydrangeas and camellias
surround my home.
All gifts left for me
by the gardener who understood
that she was planting beauty
for others to see.

In the shade and shadow
of loveliness I did not sow,
amid the Creator's décor,
I am reminded,
the garden tended with my hands
should leave splendor for
those who will follow.

"The earth's is the Lord's, and everything in it, the world, and all who live in it; for he founded it upon the seas and established it upon the waters."

—Psalm 24:1–2

Do Not Be Anxious . . .

Creation comes through God's hand,
the ocean deep, the sprawling land.
Each star that's ever lit the night
Shines in place before His sight.
He sifts the desert's wide expanse
And measures mountains with a glance.
Drops of water, big and small,
From river bank to waterfall,
Flow through the path His fingers follow,
And, still He sees each tiny sparrow.

"And even the very hairs of your head are all numbered. So don't be afraid; you are worth more than many sparrows."

—Matthew 10:30–31

A Simple Reminder

In the fading heat of day,
as dusk moves past afternoon,
the hands of God, my *Abba Father*,
trace the shape of the evening moon.

*"By wisdom the Lord laid the earth's foundations, by understanding he
set the heavens in place; by his knowledge the deeps were divided, and
the clouds let drop the dew."*

—Proverbs 3:19–20

Seasons

Flowers bloom in beds, proud of what they share;
Birds are singing sweetly; Spring is in the air.
Listen, for the chatter starts,
The song of Spring is sung,
And life is very still, as nature bears its young.
Summer has been patient, but she will wait no more;
Her arms reach through the clouds
As she opens up the door—
Her splendor is so bright; she rhymes with what I wear.
The season is for growing,
For Summer is in the air.
But Fall is on his way; he is rising hither too,
And Winter will reign in white,
When Fall is finally through!

*"There is a time for everything, and a season for every
activity under heaven."*

—Ecclesiastes 3:1

Evening Dance

Like a lovely, silver slipper,
The waxing moon dances in the sky,
Charming the darkened night,
A shoe of fantasy admired from afar.
I close my eyes and imagine
That it's waltzing with a passing star.

~

God fills my moments with music meant just for me!

~

"The Lord your God is with you, he is mighty to save.
He will take great delight in you, he will quiet you with his love, he will
rejoice over you with singing."

—Zephaniah 3:17

Sheer Beauty

God, walking with me,

Spending precious time with me,

Speaking to my heart,

Cultivating its landscape

With beauty He alone gives.

*". . . To bestow on them a crown of beauty instead of ashes, the
oil of gladness instead of mourning, and a garment of praise instead of a
spirit of despair. They will be called oaks of righteousness, a planting of
the Lord for the display of his splendor."*

—Isaiah 61:3

Growth

Crawling across my lawn,
Dampened from dusk to dawn,
Sticking to shoes and staining my toes,
Pitching tent on the patio and teasing my nose,
Filling in the nooks and corners of beds,
The greening grass of spring spreads,
Seemingly to pause in the heat of day
To flash the color that takes my breath away
—the shade of a new season.

*"One thing I ask of the Lord, this is what I seek: that I may dwell
in the house of the Lord all the days of my life, to gaze upon the beauty
of the Lord and to seek him in his temple."*

—Psalm 27:4

Flower Flight

Dandelion flight—

Pieces like paratroopers,

Falling and gliding,

Quickly, quietly to the ground,

Spreading seeds for future jumps!

"The Sovereign Lord has given me an instructed tongue, to know the word that sustains the weary. He wakens me morning by morning, wakens my ear to listen like one being taught."

—Isaiah 50:4

Frosty

A winter coat sits across my garden floor;
It crunches against my feet, marking my tread.
Chilly, I go inside . . .
Curling up at the window beside the back door,
I sit to admire the beauty stitched with icy thread.

God in His creative wonder has sewn a winter coat;
Lovely, like a luxurious cloak of cashmere,
Frozen Spanish moss drapes across the live oak's throat,
And brilliantly . . .
Long-leaf pines shimmer with snowflake chandelier.

Winter's beauty reflects God's creative wonder,
Timing, provision, and grace that never fail to amaze;
Grateful and . . .
Frosty, I ponder the thoughts within my heart that stir,
Curled up beside the Creator, through winter's long and lazy days.

*"In the beginning was the Word, and the Word was with God,
and the Word was God. He was with God in the beginning. Through
him all things were made; without him nothing was made that has been
made. In him was life, and that life was the light of men."*

—John 1:1–4

God Goes Before and Beyond the Storm

Vantage Point

> *"I know the Lord is always with me. I will not be shaken,*
> *for he is right beside me."*
>
> —Psalm 16:8 (NLT)

STORMS CAN BE RAPID-FIRE, LIFE-CHANGING experiences, and the winds that rush through them have the potential to blow fear, despair, worry, and loneliness into our lives. Learning to trust Jesus during the storms of life can be easier said than done. It's hard to trust when you feel as though everything you hold dear and precious is being blown and battered. The words describing trust roll off the tongue smoothly, but they often stick into the heart as shards of glass. In simple language, "It's hard to be steadfast in faithfulness when the waves keep rolling and you're gulping water."

However, learning to trust Jesus in the storm is not only a beautiful, personal experience, but it is also necessary for spiritual growth and maturity. Experiencing *Him* in the storm is a part of following *Him*. To know Him in the storm—to see Him halt the wind and step on top of the waves—is an unparalleled life-changing experience. Be assured, storms do not blow fear, despair, worry, or loneliness into the life of God. Learning to understand storms from God's perspective—His wisdom—is key to persevering in faith and trusting in Him. Several years ago, God used an actual storm system to teach my heart a valuable lesson.

My husband, John, and I flew out of an airport on the east coast of the United States just as a hurricane was forming off the coastline of the Atlantic. From the vantage point of the airplane's window, I had the rare opportunity to see the storm from above, and it changed my perspective.

On the ground that morning, before boarding the airplane, the air outside had been thick, moist, and hot. There was a sickly green tint to the heavens as if they were feeling nauseated and they were about to wretch! As we entered the terminal, I remember thinking how thankful I was that our plans were taking us away from the storm.

From my vantage point in the sky, the same sky appeared very different. The storm's circular shape was defined with white clouds, and its defined form was somewhat amazing to see—swirls of clouds forming together to look like a giant cinnamon roll in the sky. And, I'm not sure how to quite explain this, but the storm looked more controlled, manageable, and subject to authority. The storm's foreboding presence on the ground had changed dramatically with my view from above.

Since that day, I've lived through other life storms. And, because they are *storms*, they are by nature challenging. In truth, I've crawled through them, begged on my face through them, cried tears in the middle of them, sat in silent disbelief against their winds, and gulped my share of water as I wondered when the storm's blast would end.

I don't always handle life storms well. My first thought is not always to look for the message or the good. And, I've been known to whisper these words in prayer as the wind starts to blow: "*Oh, Jesus, please stop this . . .*"

However, God never leaves me hanging. He provides and guides. *The Bible—His Word—is my storm preparation and navigation manual.* I may not navigate life storms perfectly, but I *know* and *believe* that I am loved perfectly by God. I believe that His Word contains the truth I need to address each of my concerns, feelings, or thoughts. And I believe with all of my heart that He is Lord over the storms in my life.

I can be gulping water, and Jesus is on top of the waves.
I can be terrified, and Jesus is rebuking the wind.
I can feel like I'm going under, and His arms are wrapped securely around me.

I can be so tired that I cannot sleep, think, or eat, and Jesus is compassionate toward me.

I can feel like I'm going to drown, and His hands measure the water and sift the sand.

My feelings don't change God's nature.

Jesus is Lord; He is always in control of the storm.

And, Jesus loves me with an everlasting love.

God sees the storm in its entirety from every vantage point. In my limited sight, I see the storm from the ground, but He sees the storm from His throne. What I can see and focus on with human eyes may appear foreboding, but God may see a cinnamon roll in my life! No matter how dark or horrific it may look from where I stand, God is present. And I can trust Him completely.

I am invited and called to trust God in stormy weather. I'm invited and called to exude joy in the midst of trials. I'm invited and called to pray with a heart of gratitude in all circumstances. Admittedly, I'm still growing in this area, but my heart wants to grow. I desire to demonstrate faith that is rooted in the knowledge that God is God and I am His beloved.

I am challenged to see the storms of life through the eyes of my heart—that is the vantage point that God equips me with as I walk this earth.

Only

Only God's tender love for me,
Only His compassion for my soul,
Only His generous nature,
Only His divine character,
Only His Son's blood
Could infinitely augment grace,
As my sin increased.

*". . . But where sin increased, grace increased all the more, so that, just as
sin reigned in death, so also grace might reign through righteousness to
bring eternal life through Jesus Christ our Lord."*

—Romans 5:20–21

My Lord Walked in the Storm

Lord, I want to see You walk in the storm.

I want to see the wind *stop!* at the sound of Your voice.
Lord, I want the storm's salty spray to make me rejoice.
I want to run with You through the top of the waves.
Persevering through the storm is what my faith craves.

I want to catch the sea breeze in my hair and on my face.
Lord, in the storm's chaos, I want to find whales to chase.
I want the ocean's froth to tickle the bottom of my feet,
Developing faith that makes sea water feel like concrete.

I want to learn where the storm's treasures are hiding.
Lord, I want to be filled with Your joy both deep and
abiding.
At the sound of Your voice, I want my fear to *depart!*
Trusting You in the storm is the choice of my heart.

I want to dance on waves that toss boats like toys.
Lord, I want to hear You speak my name above the noise.
I want Your peace to weave through the storm's story,
Following You in faith and reflecting Your glory.

I want to step toward You and defy common sense.
Lord, I want water-walking feet that skip with confidence.
At the tempest's worst blast, I want to grow and transform.
Lord, the eyes of my heart can see You, and *You walked in
the storm.*

"He stilled the storm to a whisper; the waves of the sea were hushed."

—Psalm 107:29

He, for Me

The *Word of God* was questioned for me.
The *One and Only* was disrespected for me.
The *Lamb of God* was ridiculed for me.
The *Son of God* was persecuted for me.
The *King of Israel* was mocked for me.
The *Bread of Life* was broken for me.
The *Good Shepherd* was striped for me.
The *Resurrection and the Life* died for me.
The *Light* pierced the darkness for me.
All that I fully deserved . . . *Jesus* took fully for me,
Because He loves me.

"Surely he took up our infirmities and carried our sorrows, yet we considered him stricken by God, smitten by him, and afflicted. But he was pierced for our transgressions, he was crushed for our iniquities; the punishment that brought us peace was upon him, and by his wounds we are healed. We all, like sheep, have gone astray, each of us has turned to his own way; and the Lord has laid on him the iniquity of us all."
—Isaiah 53:4–6

Lamp for My Feet

In the theatre of my life

This drama has unfolded,

And, I am quite certain

That I am not equipped

To play the lead part.

~

Thankfully, my Abba Father gave me the instruction Book!

~

*"Great peace have they who love your law, and nothing
can make them stumble."*

—Psalm 119:165

Limited Sight

Today,
I was reminded that I can't see
Five seconds in front of me.
I can't predict the next eight feet
Nor guess the news my ears will greet.
I do not know the thoughts I'll feel
Or what the future might reveal.
I cannot presume where I'll tread
Nor observe the plans that lie ahead.
I've not a clue what my mirror will reflect
Or how many steps I'll need to redirect.
I cannot foresee tomorrow's weather
Nor explain details before they come together.
I may not have far-sighted sight;
All my steps ahead aren't black and white.
I surely know I'm only certain
That God in heaven is never uncertain.
And I may not predict life's entire plan,
But He planned it all before time began.
Thus to my core, with certainty,
I walk forward, believing God's in front of me.

"Your word is a lamp to my feet and a light for my path."

—Psalm 119:105

Thank You

Lord,
In weeping moments beside Your feet,
I have sought answers to questions that cannot be tamed,
Questions that storm through my system with intensity,
Leaving a channel of damage and doubt, a path of
destruction.
Like a fisherman's net, worry casts fear into my face,
And, in the putrid smell of this puzzled storm, I unravel.
Questions replace the praise on my lips, the aroma of my
joy,
And in this pit—dug so deep with the hands of my
heart—*I decompose.*
Fear steals my voice and I sit in the silence of my feelings.

It is here, in this wretched place, that You send beauty to me.
Through spring flowers dipped in the colors of heaven.
Morning upon morning, You walk beside me—
listening and loving.
My brokenness sticks into our relationship like glass;
You respond with mercy, and a song of peace plays through
my life.
*As the sun and moon take their place each day, so is Your
faithfulness to me.*

Among the lilies' velvet petals, I cease to focus on my
questions,
And in this pit—dug so deep with the hands of my
heart—*I mend.*
Grace gives me life, and I follow in the song of Your truth.

Instead of giving me all the answers, You have chosen to
give me all of Yourself.
Thank You. . . .
Thank You. . . .

"Do not let your hearts be troubled. Trust in God; trust also in me."

—John 14:1

Rain Reflections

It's been raining;
The hot humidity of late summer is thick.
Looking out the window, I'm lost in a daydream;
Coming through the storm clouds, I see
Bright, long shards of sunshine streaming through the sky,
Parting the darkened clouds like butter,
Making their way to reveal light regardless—
What an amazing picture of God's splendor, of His power.

In my heart, it's been raining,
And, with abrupt reality, I am captivated by the Creator,
The vivid imagery of His prevailing love for me
That reaches for me through fingers of grace,
Streaming through the debris of my life,
And parting cancer facades like butter,
With Light that shines through the darkest clouds of my day,
What a magnificent snapshot to keep in my heart.

~

Abba Father, abiding in Your love there is peace in the valley everyday . . . even when it rains.

~

"You will keep in perfect peace him whose mind is steadfast, because he trusts in you."

—*Isaiah 26:3*

Shelter

Abba Father,
in weary frame to this place,
I come before You now,
To grasp the breadth of Your grace
And feel Your breath upon my brow.
Abba Father,
Take my face into Your palm,
Whisper words of tender devotion
That lovingly convey the calm
And quiet the day's commotion.
Abba Father,
Carry me, close upon Your chest,
My strength to restore.
I need the security of heaven's rest;
It is the shelter I adore.

"He tends his flock like a shepherd: He gathers the lambs in his arms and carries them close to his heart; he gently leads those that have young."

—Isaiah 40:11

Pure Joy

Treasure Revealed

GOD WRITES IN MY LIFE in a manner that is His alone. No one else, no other relationship, has the capability of speaking to my heart with the volume, intensity, and precision of the Lord Almighty.

His workings in my life are not limited. Time, spatial elements, distance, frequency, circumstances, and my own sensory system—all lose their boundaries in the presence of the Creator. The sovereignty of God is revealed in His Word and established clearly in my life as He writes on my heart.

For the better part of eighteen months, I worked on a specific devotion. Its beginning had originated in the mountains of North Georgia, and everything but the ending had come with both clarity and quickness. The central message was written around the unique quality of geode rocks. My son, Jeffrey, had purchased one while on a camping trip, and God had written hundreds of words across my heart regarding the distinctive nature of these rocks and how those same qualities applied to my life. I had gladly, obediently typed the words into a devotional message; however, the ending had failed to come.

Admittedly, I was frustrated at being "stuck" regarding the ending. In multiple attempts at typing the final words, I had drawn a blank. In my prayers surrounding the message, God remained silent. It was as though He had put down His pen; therefore, in my understanding of this idea, I felt lead to follow suit, regardless of how much its incompleteness bothered me.

Then one hot day in the middle of a Utah summer, and much to my delight, God finished the devotion.

Regardless of "where" our feet are located, some things don't seem to change. Approximately 1,900 miles stretch between the red clay of the Georgia Mountains to the peculiar, rocky dirt of Antelope Island State Park in Utah (which is positioned on the Great Salt Lake). And in my experience, curious boys with vacation spending money in their pockets can locate every souvenir gift shop that exists between the two. So, once again, I found myself observing and pricing geodes and other rocks with Jeff, who, by the way, was thrilled to discover that Utah's geological structure includes geodes. I, on the other hand, was surprised at how similar they appeared to every other one I've seen. I am not educated in geology, but I didn't need an identification sticker to recognize the geodes.

I did, however, need a sticker to inform me of the price, and conveniently one was located quite visibly on the shelf. Geodes are not smooth, soothing rocks to the touch. Knowing the price and having no plans to make a personal rock purchase, I had no reason to pick one up with my own hands. I should have moved on to hat shopping. And yet I did not. Instead, I picked up a geode with my own hand.

And, as only God can, He immediately worked in my life. As my fingers wrapped around the geode, God finished the uncompleted devotion in my heart. He wrote the ending, and I could see it in big, bold paragraphs. I didn't count them, but He must have spoken a hundred words in a few seconds of time. God is sovereign; He has no limitations or restrictions.

My loving Father's message spanned the time of eighteen months and crossed the distance of eight states. He waited until my feet stood on desert soil to speak a beautiful message on brokenness to my heart. He gave me the concrete experience of the desert to better understand the immeasurability of His love. He has perfect timing.

For the vacation days that followed, I could see His splendor among the colors and patterns that only the desert conditions produce.

In reflection, I am reminded that God always teaches me beyond the words that He gives me to write. What I saw as an unfinished piece of writing, God saw as a developing piece of *heartwork*. And so it is with the various trials of life. What I see as a time of difficulty, distance, or confusion, God sees as an opportunity to deepen and anchor my faith. What I see as a storm, God sees as a reflecting pool for His joy.

Original Devotion:

A few months ago, Jeff bought a geode rock from a souvenir shop in the mountains of North Georgia. Earlier in the day, he had spent several hours picking up smooth, free-of-charge stones from the creek that ran alongside our campsite. So I was little surprised that he would spend his vacation money on a rock, much less a rock that looked so craggy and dull on the outside. I asked him in the store if he knew "what" it was. He quickly replied, "Oh yeah, there's treasure inside this rock." Having addressed my question, he made his purchase.

When we returned home, he placed the geode on the back porch alongside the oval rocks gathered from the creek. The geode clearly looked out of place. The creek stones, smooth and polished from years of being washed in the water, shimmered in the sunlight, and the beautiful colors of the water were revealed in their surface. In comparison, the geode resembled a petrified meatball—lumpy, round, and dull. And when the light touched its surface, it looked like a rock.

My interest piqued, I continued to be surprised when

Jeff did not attempt to break open the geode. After all, he is an eleven-year-old boy and they are known for showing keen interest in any activity involving smashing items with a hammer. However, when I asked him about it, he simply replied, "No, I think I'll leave it just like this. I know there is treasure inside."

Apparently, I wasn't the only one perplexed. Molly, our Labrador, tried to eat the thing, only to fail, and resorted to playing with it like a ball for a couple of days. (As a side note, Labradors are known to attempt to eat anything—even rocks!) John tried to throw it in the garbage after labeling it more trash than treasure and appeared dumbstruck when I reminded him that Jeff had paid good money for this rock.

One day after my toes had accidentally found it in the grass, I insisted that Jeff "do something" with his rock. His solution to my suggestion was a new-found interest in attempting to break it open.

It was at this point that we speculated that perhaps geodes are truly petrified, because the outer surface was very hard to break. However, eleven-year-old boys are also known to be determined. And, finally, after many swings of the hammer, the surface cracked and the rock broke open.

I forget the words that came from Jeff's mouth, but I remember his expression—delight. Delight traced the lines of his face and rested in the corners of his smile as what he

had known all along came into plain view on my back porch. The hammer's blow had transformed the craggy, dull outer surface of the geode into a backdrop for the most remarkable, iridescent crystals, crystals so lovely that our breath was held hostage for a few seconds as our eyes took in their beauty— extraordinary inside the ordinary, reflecting the colors of the desert and appearing to dance with the light.

Jeff, confident in his purchase all along, placed the broken pieces of the rock on our coffee table. No one in my home questioned his decision. The rock, rendered so by the brokenness, now revealed its worth and value.

I find it non-coincidental as I study and pray through the journey of trials and the instructions revealed in the book of James that I find myself researching information on geode rocks. My Jesus, if anything, is ever-creative, always teaching, and consistently using the ordinary in my life to reveal truth.

So, what have I learned about geodes? More than you might like to know, but several facts are noteworthy:

- Each geode is unique in composition.
- Geodes can only be truly discovered when cracked open.
- The size and formation of crystals and different shades of color within the crystals make each geode special.

- The rough exterior of the geode gives no indication of the secrets held within its core.
- Geodes are found throughout the world, but the most concentrated areas are located in the deserts.
- The term geode is derived from the Greek word Geoides, which means "earthlike."[1]

Earthlike. That word, much like a rock, lands heavy on my heart. Recurrent tears begin to stop. I'm suddenly taken aback that God shows up in my life every day, all the time, and in the most creative ways. I'm deliberating His wisdom, His love, and His grandeur while my fingers toy with a piece of three-dollar rock. God is the best teacher. And with the precision of a surgeon, He touches the exact place in my heart that wrestles against Him. You're probably familiar with that place. It is a very *earthlike* place. In my own life, I've nicknamed it "why."

At times in my relationship with God, I've whined, cried, and begged to be free from certain trials. I have frequently asked God a version of three questions, each beginning with the word "why." "Why is this happening? Why won't You stop this trial? Why do I have to spend time in the

---

1. "Geodes," http://www.desertusa.com/magjan98/jan_pap/du_rock_ge-ode.html (accessed October 26, 2011).

desert?" Sound familiar? I'm guessing you have your own personalized version. These types of questions echo my *earthlike nature*—my grip on the control button of my life. Following the footsteps of Jesus requires me to release that grip and surrender the control button or the hammer into His capable, loving hands.

God is able to use the brokenness that weaves its way through my life to reveal the treasure of His abiding presence and His nature. My heart can be filled with *pure joy* through various trials because God is *pure joy* and He never leaves my side.

I may be temporarily contained to an earth suit, but my life is not earthlike. I am a dearly loved, adored child of God, and my heart, filled with all the presence of the Almighty, is brimming with treasure.

Summer Day

Sun-kissed summer tan

Falling across my pale cheeks,

Delighting my smile,

Painting my face with color,

Pulling the joy from my heart.

Sun-kissed summer tan

Filling my face with wonder,

Creating a grin,

Building laughter with my Lord,

Pulling the praise from my heart.

"I am coming to you now, but I say these things while I am still in the world, so that they may have the full measure of my joy within them."

—John 17:13

Summer 2009

The sun in beating, summer heat
warms the dirt beneath my feet
and bids me pause to just perceive
the blessings rich that I receive.
The sunny days against my face
pop my freckles into place.
My toes relax in ocean sand,
gardening soil stains my hand.
The brilliant sun in splendor bright
stirs my giggle of delight,
While summer's bounty at its best
pulls the praise from my chest.
A scar could never fade the sweet
of laughter locked in summer's heat.

"Trust in the Lord with all your heart and lean not on your own understanding; in all your ways acknowledge him, and he will make your paths straight."

—Proverbs 3:5–6

Blueberry Thoughts

My hair feels sticky; my skin feels sticky; bug spray fills my
nose.
Warm dirt shifts underneath my feet; flip-flops expose my
toes.
My eyes fill with color—countless orbs of deep blue
Sparkling in sunlight still covered in morning dew.
My fingers splotch; I look like I've been playing in ink.
Antioxidant-packed-fruit; underneath the blue, they must
be pink!
Lattice-like patterns of sweat trickle down my back.
My heart skips a beat; my lips start to smack.
I'm happy; I'm hooked; I'm filled with delight;
Grabbing a big handful, I prepare to take a big bite.

Blueberries burst,
And the taste of summer fills my mouth.

*"May the words of my mouth and the meditation of my heart be pleasing
in your sight, O Lord, my Rock and my Redeemer."*

—Psalm 19:14

Joy

Beneath the live oak's winding frame,
A barefoot little boy swings,
His feet extending to touch the sky,
The space between us filled with his laughter.
Spring's carefree attitude displayed in the childhood game,
Too soon his interest will give way to other things,
But the sugared memory of play will last long after
His imagination stops believing he can fly.
—Head back; hair messy—
Today, the tire swing is calling his name,
And his toes reach for the tall tree's rafters.

"The Lord bless you and keep you; the Lord make his face shine upon you and be gracious to you; the Lord turn his face toward you and give you peace."

—Numbers 6:24–26

Heartsease

Digging underneath these aged trees,
I sense the *Gardener's* loving presence,
And I feel Him pull me tight and squeeze.
Working here among the floral essence,
I inhale the measure of divine heartsease.

"...And surely I am with you always, to the very end of the age."

—Matthew 28:20

Coastal Joy

Salty air, hot sand,
Water covering my toes,
Fingers moving shells,
Fiddler crabs playing nearby,
Wind reordering my hair.
What a good day!

"The Word became flesh and made his dwelling among us. We have seen his glory, the glory of the One and Only, who came from the Father, full of grace and truth."

—John 1:14

Innovative Thinking

How can the aroma of spring make . . .
My steps seem lighter?
My wintry mood brighter?
My flower beds composed?
My pale skin exposed?
My afternoon energy longer?
My cleaning mood stronger?
My flip-flops innovative fashion?
My day lily garden a passion?
How can the aroma of spring . . .
Revolutionize these things?
I don't really know,
But it's a change I'll happily take!

"They will come and shout for joy on the heights of Zion; they will re-joice in the bounty of the Lord—the grain, the new wine and the oil, the young of the flocks and herds. They will be like a well-watered garden, and they will sorrow no more."

—Jeremiah 31:12

Sassy Cat

Lizards green,
Barely seen,
Skirt between my feet.
Callygirl cat
Will have no part of that;
She stalks them for a treat!
Lizards quick
Dart to trick
My eyes from seeing.
Callygirl cat
Appears to ignore that,
But her claws are disagreeing!
Lizards flee
At the sight of me,
Or is it from my sweet feline?
Callygirl cat,
So sassy and fat,
Is anything but benign!

"Then one of the elders said to me, 'Do not weep! See, the Lion of the tribe of Judah, the Root of David, has triumphed. He is able to open the scroll and its seven seals."

—Revelation 5:5

Summer Psychotherapy

Cocooned in the hammock, I dangle,
Entrapped by the tree canopy's charms;
Unwinding in the afternoon garden, I untangle,
Swinging in summer's sticky arms.

Mood metamorphosis—therapy in a rope cot;
Stress fades, grass grows, flowers bloom.
This woven cradle is my favorite spot
And it's suspended in my favorite room.

*"Love must be sincere. Hate what is evil; cling to what is good. Be devoted to one
another in brotherly love. Honor one another above yourselves. Never be lacking
in zeal, but keep your spiritual fervor, serving the Lord. Be joyful in hope, pa-
tient in affliction, faithful in prayer."*

—Romans 12:9–12

Summer Charm

In the growing heat of late May,
Fresh summer corn and pink-eyed peas
Romance my senses and buckle my knees,
Leading my southern mouth to open wide and say,
"Fix me a plate, please!"

"Then Jesus declared, 'I am the bread of life. He who comes to me will never go hungry, and he who believes in me will never be thirsty."

—John 6:35

Springtime Pillow

Warm air mixing with freshly cut grass,
Creating an aroma that lingers in my hair;
Inhaling a long, deep breath, I pass
My cat, posing as a cushion in my wicker chair.

The passing spring sky a brilliant blue,
Daffodils unfurl, forming dainty basins for rain,
While jasmine tendrils reach toward where they're crawling to;
Against June's sun, May cannot complain.

Spring precedes summer down the season's aisle,
Sleeping underneath the long-leaf pines tonight;
I dream of tomorrow's beauty, and for a brief, precious while,
My eyes close to see the unfolding color of summer's light.

My tousled curls impinging on my pillow case the smell of
spring.

"I was there when he set the heavens in place, when he marked out
the horizon on the face of the deep, when he established the clouds above
and fixed securely the fountains of the deep, when he gave the sea
its boundary so the waters would not overstep his command, and
when he marked out the foundations of the earth."

—*Proverbs 8:27–29*

Peace

My Father, the Gardener,
In misty morning and moments tender,
Unfolds the day lily's velvety splendor.
Blooms appear in heat of day and sun so bright;
They disappear with moon's first light,
With sturdy scape and petal frail,
The lilies grow as worries fail.
In petals sprinkled with morning's dew,
They greet the day with beauty new.
In the Vine—abiding—my heart can know
The life of peace *wherein the lilies grow.*

"Who of you by worrying can add a single hour to his life? And why do you worry about clothes? See how the lilies of the field grow. They do not labor or spin. Yet I tell you that not even Solomon in all his splendor was dressed like one of these."

—Matthew 6:27–29

God, the Cleaner of My Heart

Search Me and Know Me

FRIEND, SOMETIMES DEBRIS BLOWS INTO your life and leaves you wondering if your world has just spun off its axis. When that happens, it is my experience that God is the only One who can come in, sweep it all up, brush the scope of your emotions into a dustpan, and then dump it *all* somewhere far, far away from your heart. While it may be awkward to think of the Almighty as a custodian, it is elemental for us to understand that He is the *cleaner of our hearts*. And we should be filled with gratitude that He is not only able but also willing to address the dirt and debris—the real life junk—that litters our lives. In Psalm 139:23–24, David wrote, "Search me, O God, and know my heart; test me and know my anxious thoughts. See if there is any offensive way in me, and lead me in the way everlasting."

My own heart needs daily cleaning, and the collection of junk that lines my day is reflected in my journal. Thoughts and feelings often collide to form something less than

Christ-like. Jeremiah 17:9 says, "The heart is deceitful above all things and beyond cure. Who can understand it?" God understands it. And although He frequently has to take a mop and a broom to my life, I am continually humbled that He deals with my heart straightaway with mercy and grace. The words below are from an entry in my journal. It happened to be my birthday, but it could have been any ordinary day:

17, March

It's my birthday; no one has school today; I have no place to be today at any given time; my alarm clock is off; and although sleeping late is one of my very favorite things to do—I AM WIDE AWAKE! In fact, I was wide awake around 5:15 this morning. The one day of the year I could probably sleep as long as I like without complaint or threat, and my body doesn't comply.

Actually, it's my heart that is refusing to comply. My heart has been slightly tangled and strangled lately. As thoughts and situations collide, I have found myself packed with feelings—feelings that don't always sit well across the heart. And, as much as I regret to admit this, I have been a very poor manager of my stress!

Even as I sit striking keys, a bad case of shingles runs down my back and across my stomach. Yucky, painful,

*annoying virus . . . gone haywire in my system due to
stress! They are healing, but they have been disruptive to
say the least. Consequently, I've been talking to God A
LOT about my stress. The Maker of heaven and earth
has the skinny on my inner thoughts! Be assured, the
Almighty has been given the whole list of things that upset
me, bother me, rush me, frustrate me, embarrass me, annoy
me, overwhelm me, anger me, etc. etc. etc. . . . I have whined,
and wallowed, and wished A LOT lately.*

*I am ever-grateful that God loves me; that no matter how
disorganized, dim, complicated, small, or temporary my
thoughts, He listens. My heart does not have a corner His
eyes cannot see. I don't experience feelings His compassion
cannot touch. I don't live through a moment when He is
not present. God can know my inner thoughts and adore
me deeply with a love that reaches long and wide, high
and deep! He is my "Abba Father," and this morning, He
whispered 2 words across my stressed-out heart:*

Follow Me

*He could have spoken to every detail of every thought
and situation. He could have sent me a flow chart of stress
management from heaven. He could have given me books,
or pie, or flowers. He could have shown up with an apron,
a tool belt, or a hard hat, because it's not like I haven't*

*wanted Him to "fix" some things lately. He could have
ignored me. God could have done or said anything. But,
He loves me. . . . And He knew exactly what I needed,
what my heart most longed for this morning . . .*

Him . . . just Him!

*So, bearing the stress marks of a life not so well managed,
I put one foot in front of the other and walk forward . . .
finding myself among the beloved, redeemed children of
God who call themselves followers of Christ. We are not a
perfect bunch, but we are loved—so dearly loved!*

If I love God with all my heart, then I give Him access to
all my heart. In other words, in my relationship with Him,
the "Do Not Disturb" sign should never hang on the door
of my heart.

Summer Development

Summer flowers flirt with my senses,
Filling my life with color and wonder,
Inviting conversation and breaking down my defenses.
Among my inner thoughts, *the Gardener* will plunder,
Loving me and addressing all my pretenses,
Forming a whole, devoted heart that is His . . .
A vessel filled with thanksgiving.

*"Love the Lord your God with all your heart and with all your soul and
with all your strength."*

—Deuteronomy 6:5

Psalm 139 Moment

Am I Pretentious?
Malicious?
Filled with Envious,
Devious Thoughts?
Am I Mean? Unkind?
First in my Mind?
Am I Impatient?
Overspent?
Careless,
Or Word Reckless?
Am I Anxious or Rash?
Do my Motives Clash?
Can I Give Cheerfully?
Is My Life All about Me?

Search My Heart, Lord,
And Tell Me . . .

"Search me, O God, and know my heart; test me and know my anxious thoughts."

—Psalm 139:23

Vast Is the Peace

Rotting stench, the trial's debris can be my heart's dictator.
Confused, afraid, and way too full of my own feelings,
Exhausted, I find myself tossed from wave to wave;
Desperate and disordered, my thoughts are reeling.
Struggling against the personal groundswell, I cave,
Crawling into Your lap and giving into the wisdom You
offer,
The insight You provide.
Lord, when I cease to fight the chaos trials can stir
And I become obediently surrendered by Your side,
I am immediately calmed, as the Galilean wind that knew
its Creator.

~

Abba Father, vast is the peace that follows trusting in You.
Keep the eyes of my heart secured on Your face.

~

"...*Then he stood up and told the wind to be silent, the sea to quiet
down: 'Silence!' The sea became smooth as glass. The men rubbed their
eyes, astonished. 'What's going on here? Wind and sea come to heel at
his command!'*"

—Matthew 8:26–27 (The Message)

HeartWork

Debris decorates my heart
Like grandstands at a parade;
Tears caught in my throat,
Emotions overloaded,
I need a divine spring cleaning,
I need a mental yard sale,
I need to do my HeartWork.

*"Still others, like seed sown among thorns, hear the word; but the worries
of this life, the deceitfulness of wealth and the desires for other things
come in and choke the word, making it unfruitful. Others, like seed sown
on good soil, hear the word, accept it, and produce a crop—thirty, sixty or
even a hundred times what was sown."*

—Mark 4:18–20

Time in a Mason Jar

Lord, I need to hear You speak my name,
I need to run my toes through spring grass,
Discovering Your beauty and peace.

I hear my lips mouthing the hurried prayer
That I won't let this morning pass
Without first devouring time with You.

My heart halts, the busy fails to cease;
Time cannot be captured in a jar of glass.
Sitting, I must choose to spend time with You.

~

Lord, I open Your Word and pour another cup of coffee. . . .

~

"Very early in the morning, while it was still dark, Jesus got up, left the house and went off to a solitary place, where he prayed."

—Mark 1:35

Surrendered

Lord, calm me and create a new heart in me;
Slow my breathing,
Guide me to endure, knowing that You are conceiving
And weaving a beautiful tapestry
With a pattern that I will one day see.
Lord, use the dark threads that lie on the path before me.
My days, these moments, belong to You;
I am surrendered to the purpose You are achieving.

"Do not conform any longer to the pattern of this world, but be trans-
formed by the renewing of your mind. Then you will be able to test and
approve what God's will is—his good, pleasing and perfect will."

—Romans 12:2

Breakfast on the Shore

Like Peter, I want to dive off of the boat and swim to the
shore;
I want to love You and follow You forevermore.

When my heart is breaking and broken
And weighed down by things both known and unspoken,
When my guilt is all I can taste and my failure is all I can
see,
I want to find You by the fire making breakfast for me.

Time, I need time with Jesus—my friend and my Lord.
Like Peter, I want a life transformed and a heart restored!

*"Then the disciple whom Jesus loved said to Peter, 'It is the Lord!' As
soon as Simon Peter heard him say, 'It is the Lord,' he wrapped his outer
garment around him (for he had taken it off) and jumped into the water."*
—John 21:7

"The third time he said to him, 'Simon son of John, do you love me?'
Peter was hurt because Jesus asked him the third time, 'Do you love me?'
He said, 'Lord, you know all things; you know that I love you.' Jesus
said, 'Feed my sheep.'"

—John 21:17

Writer's Heart

In the garden,
God's tender care evinces,
Filling my soul,
Flooding my senses,
Lifting praise from my lips
And words of adoration from my pen.

"If you have any encouragement from being united with Christ, if any comfort from his love, if any fellowship with the Spirit, if any tenderness and compassion, then make my joy complete by being like-minded, having the same love, being one in spirit and purpose."

—Philippians 2:1–2

King Jesus Washed My Feet

The splendor of the room reaches beyond measure.
Brilliant light reflects in precious jewels and treasure.
The music playing is the loveliest sound in creation,
The beauty of each detail displaying divine imagination.
Rulers and peasants alike worship before the mercy seat.
Around the throne, a chorus of angels in sacred song repeat:
"Holy, Holy, Holy is the Lord God Almighty
Who was, and is, and is to come!"
In heaven's light, I stand on the temple floor bringing
nothing
And receive Everything . . .
Because my feet have been washed by the King.

"One thing I ask of the Lord, this is what I seek: that I may dwell in the
house of the Lord all the days of my life, to gaze upon the beauty of the
Lord and to seek him in his temple."

—Psalm 27:4

Sticky Word

Certain words, as if laced with honey,
Stick in my throat.
Sipping a glass of sweet tea
Helps tremendously.
However, some words simply stick.
And my heart, so desperately sick,
must tell my throat to produce more spit.
Suffering is one of those words for me.
Like salt, it dries my mouth as if draining the sea.
And my heart, so capable of deception,
must yield completely to the Lord's careful inspection.
The arid, adhesive effect His words refute.
I know *suffering* is just a sticky word,
but beyond doubt,
It has the tendency to turn my mouth inside-out!
And my heart, capable of dehydrating, can follow suit.

"The heart is deceitful above all things and beyond cure.
Who can understand it?"

—Jeremiah 17:9

My Ever-present Helper

Understanding Trust

I CAN ONLY SPEAK FOR myself, but when I am in trouble, I want immediate help! And my cries for help are not always pretty, nor are they eloquent or even clearly defined. In truth, they are most often ugly, rugged, and raw in nature; they are the guts of the garbage that can pile up within me. Perhaps you are wired the same way? How restful and reassuring to know that God understands our very basic need for help, and how comforting and encouraging to know that He is ever-present.

It's not easy to expose your guts to others. It's risky. But, God leads my inner parts—my heart—to trust Him and to be courageous. Along that line of thought, I've lost count of the heart lessons that I've acquired sitting beside the wrestling mat. If you are familiar with the sport, then you will understand that there is a lot of waiting that takes place. Gratefully, God has used that time to teach my heart, and I wrote the following entry in my journal after wrestling with my own understanding of fear, worry, and God's ever-present help. The truth of these words still holds steadfast:

> *Recently, while teaching through the Gospel of John, I was asked a difficult question regarding fear and worry. Basically, this question was posed: "Do you believe that all worry is sin?" It should have been an easy answer, but in truth, I scrambled for words.*
>
> *As I left that day, I couldn't shake a collage of questions that were beginning to piece themselves over my heart. Was all worry sin? And, if so, then why did I worry about anything? Why did I ever experience anxiety or fear or worry? If I trust the words of Jesus, then why do I live like I do not? Do I really believe He is capable of taking care of me? Do I really trust Him?*
>
> *Ah! The* trust *word. Over the last year, trust had become a resounding theme in my relationship with God. Driving home from study that day, I knew that God was teaching me a new lesson in trust, and the next week I conducted a word analysis of the word* worry.
>
> *God is a good teacher. My search brought new meaning and new head knowledge to my understanding of worry. When dissected, the composition of the word* worry *reveals words and phrases such as "choke," "strangle," "snapping at the throat," and "aggressive attack."*

In a nutshell, through my word study, I came to a deeper and more educated understanding that whenever I choose to worry and hold on to fear and anxiety, I am giving Satan permission to choke me, to bite at me, and to tear at me with his teeth.

Not exactly a pretty scene to visualize! And, certainly not something to which I would subject myself.

So, why do I worry?

Why do you?

For me, the answer lies not within my understanding of worry but rather in my understanding of trust.

God is not only a good teacher, but He is also the best teacher. Within a week of my new-found head knowledge concerning worry, God went straight for my heart lesson on trust. He is always more invested in my heart-work than my head knowledge. God does not call us away from worry without calling us toward trusting Him. It is within the framework of a trusting relationship with Jesus that we discover the peace that surpasses our understanding and eclipses our circumstances.

". . . The Lord is near. Do not be anxious about anything, but in everything, by prayer and petition, with thanksgiving, present your requests to God. And the peace of God, which transcends all understanding, will guard your hearts and your minds in Christ Jesus."

—Philippians 4:5–7

"Don't fret or worry. Instead of worrying, pray. Let petitions and praises shape your worries into prayers, letting God know your concerns. Before you know it, a sense of God's wholeness, everything coming together for good, will come and settle you down. It's wonderful what happens when Christ displaces worry at the center of your life."

—Philippians 4:6–7 (The Message)

"Trust in the Lord with all your heart and lean not on your own understanding; in all your ways acknowledge him, and he will make your paths straight."

—Proverbs 3:5–6

I believe that our identity as God's children creates a longing inside our hearts to be free from worry. Most of us desire to live without the chokehold of fear. Just as our own children long to know that we can protect and keep them, we desire the same from Jesus. A daily decision to trust with our heart deepens our assurance that God is our protector and our ever-present help in times of trouble.

God desires to help me; God will help me; God lovingly gives me permission to cry out to Him—and to ask for help.

Heart Threads

Lord, my thoughts, uncertain of a destination,
Wander to entangle,
Forming a chaotic pattern of frustration,
Leading my flesh and my mind to wrangle
With Your pierced, guiding hand.
Like spilled ink, doubt and fear quickly spread,
Staining the moments this hour has spanned.
Lord, unravel the thoughts of my heart,
As if You're pulling a loosened thread.

"Do not be quick with your mouth, do not be hasty in your heart to utter anything before God. God is in heaven and you are on earth, so let your words be few."

—Ecclesiastes 5:2

His Touch

If not for God's closeness,
His presence,
His Word, and His grace,
His rugged hand upon my face,
The painful darkness of this wasteland
Would have left my heart sightless.

"Jesus answered, 'I am the way and the truth and the life. No one comes to the Father except through me.'"

—John 14:6

Loss Song

Through loss overwhelming,
I am lovingly, gently comforted;
The tender mercy of God's provision
Behests my grieving heart to sing,
And I am shadowed
With a song of thanksgiving.

*"The Lord is close to the brokenhearted and saves those who are crushed
in spirit. A righteous man may have many troubles, but the Lord delivers
him from them all."*

—Psalm 34:18–19

God of Comfort

Lord, comfort comes and covers me
And cloaks my heart completely;
I hear You sing a song of love
Into my slumber sweetly.
Immersed within Your care,
Your sheltering arms abide
To keep me safe and ever-close
Within the peace that You provide.

Lord, comfort comes and covers me
And fills my life with rest;
I hear You whisper words of love
Across the scars upon my chest.
Surrounded by Your strength,
Your mercy floods my soul
And leads my feet to follow You
Because I know You're in control.

Lord, comfort comes and covers me
And speaks to my deepest need;
I hear You tell my mind to still
And to Your will accede.
Encircled in Your divine embrace,
Your compassion ever sweet

Brings my all to trust in You
For life that You alone replete.

"Praise be to the God and Father of our Lord Jesus Christ, the Father of compassion and the God of all comfort, who comforts us in all our troubles, so that we can comfort those in any trouble with the comfort we ourselves have received from God. For just as the sufferings of Christ flow over into our lives, so also through Christ our comfort overflows."

2 Corinthians 1:3–5

In All Seasons

In all seasons, God, the Great Shepherd, leads.
He walks before me with strength and courage.
He holds me close to His heart and gives me rest.
He is my ever-present help in times of need.

He sits encircled above the earth, and my voice reaches His
ears.
With gentleness, He cradles the concerns of my life in His
hands.
Each of my mornings finds His mercies ever new.
His presence calms my mind and quiets my fears.

I walk in the shadow of His wings.
While I rest, He watches over me.
He adores me; He blesses me; He is faithful.
My heart is filled with a song that He alone sings.

He is bigger than any problem I face.
He is enough.
From Everlasting to Everlasting, He is God.
I recline into His fully sufficient grace.

Nothing is too hard for Him . . . no issue; no problem; no
malady.

His voice commands the oceans and rebukes the wind.
He is Lord over this storm in my life.
In all seasons, God, the Great Shepherd, leads me.

"I am the good shepherd; I know my sheep and my sheep know me."

—John 10:14

The Pen to My Life

My heart breaking, I have come to this place time and time
again.
Lord, my hand could not write the story that You have
written
Across the moments of my life. You author my steps—each
one.
I can dive headfirst into despair—rendering myself unglued
and undone.
Circumstances can leave me confused and doubting. I can
swim in distress—
How amazed I am that in these moments, You don't love
me any less.
In grief, I have wondered if You knew or cared where my
thoughts came from.
In response, You speak in gentle boldness of the promises
that are to come.
I can follow my own heart and think some ugly thoughts
and notions.
I can wring my hands in despair and I can be the queen of
emotions.
The numbing nature of pain temporarily blinds me to
seeing the path provided.
Even as my feet stumble, I know that I cannot follow a
heart that is divided.
I was called and invited to follow You; You called my name.

You step ahead of me.

My heart and my feet touch no place that You cannot find or understand or see.

You write a story of redeeming love in the wilderness, on the mountain, in the valley.

When the sun shines or when the storm blows, I will always find You beside me.

Some put their hope in chariots, some in horses; some place it in mere men.

Lord, I choose to put my hope in You; I surrender the pages of my life, and also the pen.

"Some trust in chariots and some in horses, but we trust in the name of the Lord our God. They are brought to their knees and fall, but we rise up and stand firm."

—Psalm 20:7–8

Grace

Jesus kneels to write, her shame apparent.
Guilt, like a thick curtain, darkens the crowd.
Did her eyes find the rocks, when Jesus bent?
Did she flinch? Did the accusers laugh aloud?
Was her life so disposable, so inconsequential?
Did no one else offer sympathy or understanding?
Onlookers gathered, expecting to witness a stoning, until
Jesus stands and speaks the words that leave no one standing
To accuse her anymore.

Grace abounding . . .
Compassion astounding . . .

Jesus kneels, writing in the dust, the divine hand of God
tracing the dirt.
A story of love beyond measure, both redeeming and overt.
This is the story of the lost, the daughter Jesus came for.

". . . But Jesus bent down and started to write on the ground with his finger.
When they kept on questioning him, he straightened up and said to them,
'If any one of you is without sin, let him be the first to throw a stone at her.'
Again he stooped down and wrote on the ground."

—John 8:6–8

Come, Lord

Come, Lord, and walk with me,
be my close companion today.
Open my eyes to the beauty of Your creation,
let me breathe in Your majesty along my way.
Listen to the voice of my heart
and quiet my doubts and fear.
Touch my face with Your hand,
wrap Your arms around me, draw me near.
Allow Your splendor to bring praise into my life,
and cloak me with Your presence as I discover Your peace.
Only You know my need for healing,
and only You understand the depth of my grief.
Because of You, I am transformed; I am loved and cherished
forever,
as Deep calls to deep; this is my heart's belief.
Come, Lord, and walk with me,
be my close companion today.

"Deep calls to deep in the roar of your waterfalls; all your waves and breakers have swept over me. By day the Lord directs his love, at night his song is with me—a prayer to the God of my life."

—Psalm 42:7–8

Flower Talk

Watering my flowers this morning,
I found myself sharing
Dreams and worries, thoughts and fears,
Conversation reflecting changes made through
the years,
Going through chores, ideas, and appointments,
I'm thankful that nothing I said had to make sense;
I've learned the flowers keep my words in
confidence.
Displaying beauty surrounded by aged trees
And cuddling with weeds that grow where they
please,
They hear the quiet click and creak of my aged
knees.
I water and speak openly about the hot, humid day,
I water and speak lovingly about the dogs at play,
I water and discuss the promise of summer showers,
Letting the sprinklers sing as I converse with my
flowers.
Satisfying their thirsty throats, I soak them lavishly,
Rewarded by blooms speaking love language to me;
In their beauty, the beauty of God is all I can see.
Simply managing the sprinklers, I simply talk and pray;
As words like water drops fall, I know the Creator listens
today.

Watering His flowers this morning,
I found God sharing.

"... The Lord is the everlasting God, the Creator of the ends of the earth.
He will not grow tired or weary, and his understanding no one can fath-
om. He gives strength to the weary and increases the power of the weak.
Even youths grow tired and weary, and young men stumble and fall; but
those who hope in the Lord will renew their strength. They will soar on
wings like eagles; they will run and not grow weary, they will walk and
not be faint."

—Isaiah 40:28–31

Lord of All

Lord of All

IF THERE IS A SECTION of this book that bears the challenge of my heart to trust in God, it would be this chapter. Here, pages apart, are the poems "Why" and "Carried." The thoughts and emotion poured forth in their message accurately express the confusion my heart can experience. Deeply, I believe the rich, unshakeable truth reflected in "Carried." I hold the truth of Deuteronomy 33:12 near and dear; the truth of the verse is written on my heart. Yet, I have also spewed back my share of doubt, confusion, and pain into the Lord's lap as reflected in the poem "Why." I am so grateful for my *Abba Father* who loves me enough to hold me close to His chest even as I whine, vent, or puke up the worst of my heart.

God never changes, and He is always my Father. He is Lord of All—all feelings, all thoughts, all the moments of my day. I have discovered that I both want and need a *Big God*. I need a God who can understand me! I want a God who is *Lord of All* and also my *dad*. I want a God who makes me laugh. I want a God who understands my love for blueberries. I need a God who not only knows what I ate for breakfast but is also interested in what I'm cooking for dinner. And, I want a God who walks among the lilies with me. Thankfully, I have a God who is *all those things and so much more* than my heart desires. He is so very amazing.

You, Almighty God,
Whose fingers trace the shape of the evening moon,
And whose thoughts pull forth the lily's color,
Love me!
With a love that is faithful and uniquely mine.
You see every moment of my day—
You understand my feelings—
You listen to thoughts I cannot even put into words—
You intercede for me.
You welcome me to sit on the floor of Your throne room,
To rest on the pallet You lay for me at Your feet.
You keep me close.
But today, just because You love me—
You pull me up and into Your lap,
Into the arms that reached for me,
And You hold me close for as long as I need to be held.

You are my Abba Father—
You are Lord of All—Lord of my life!

Ocean Therapy

Blue waves tickle my hand
Beside the temperate sea;
My crinkled toes sift the sand,
And God sits with me.
Fiddler crabs skirt the water;
Full of thoughts and thanksgiving,
I am quiet with wonder.
My cells brim with abundant living,
My skin soaking up God's amazing sun.
The hot, heat floods through me,
And I am drawn to the fun
Of feeling His strength
Through the ocean beneath me.

"But blessed is the man who trusts in the Lord, whose confidence is in him. He will be like a tree planted by the water that sends out its roots by the stream. It does not fear when heat comes; its leaves are always green. It has no worries in a year of drought and never fails to bear fruit."

—Jeremiah 17:7–8

Carried

The worries of life are held at bay,
His breathe upon the brow,
Close to His heart, the cradled lamb,
Nestles in to stay,
To hear the refrain; the song of grace,
The loving Shepherd will sing,
To the sheep who rest,
Upon His chest,
Close to their beloved King.

". . . Let the beloved of the Lord rest secure in him, for he shields him all day long, and the one the Lord loves rests between his shoulders."

—Deuteronomy 33:12

Blue Skies

The wilderness—damp and cold mixed with heat and
humidity,
Elements of guilt, grief, sorrow, distress, and moments of
stupidity
Line this path of wasteland, this dry desert, this barren place.
Elements harsh etch my heart, as difficulty lines my face.
On my own I am crushed here; I cannot stand to prevail
Against the blast of trouble's wind and gust of stormy gale.
I fall to beg; on my hands and knees I plead; I shatter.
In heart, I query if the lessons here will ever really matter,
And then God speaks in wisdom full to my full uncertainty;
Straight to my heart, His question lands, *"Child, are you
questioning me?"*

I don't want to; I want to stand; I want to persevere; I want
to fail to break,
But in this grief, this wasteland bare, I've walked in misery's
wake.
I am done . . . I am undone . . . God is the only One who
can provide
The imparted path beneath my feet where joy and peace
abide.
In heart, I know I've lost my footing, and my mind is
gripped in fear.

In labored minutes of anguish faced, my *Abba Father* draws
near;
He whispers, *"Dear child,"* . . . and then gives a thousand
words to me,
His message: *"To stand in perseverance here, you must depend on
Me."*
His words pierce the shadow of my night's darkness with
light;
My wounds are dressed with balm; my blindness gives way
to sight.

Amid the darkness cloaked in the dark, my heart can see to
stand;
I find the Way, along my way, in broken, sun-scorched land.
I follow in the rain, the wind, the gusty blast of wasteland
heat;
I'll follow Christ on my hands and knees, if I falter on my
feet.
In heart, I know that desert skies don't fade to blue sky
dreams;
Not fantasy but reality provides my footing for tested faith
it seems.
Neither one cloud moves, nor rains forget to fall; the desert
dust remains.
Everything—all of it—can crash around me, but my Lord

will stay the same.
In broken steps and broken heart, I've learned the
wilderness can be
My place where faith stands in my Father; and my sky is as
blue as the sea.

*". . . The Lord is near. Do not be anxious about anything, but in every-
thing, by prayer and petition, with thanksgiving, present your requests
to God. And the peace of God, which transcends all understanding, will
guard your hearts and your minds in Christ Jesus."*

Philippians 4:5–7

Branches

Bending over my head,
Beautiful—
Dancing, slowly
Courted by the flirtatious wind,
The twisted arms of brown and green
Shade my thoughts quietly,
Buffering the din of my tears,
Parting slightly, and only to let my laughter escape.
These timeworn branches
My sentiments have seen,
And beneath this tree, God has heard the prayers I've said.

"He has showed you O man, what is good. And what does the Lord
require of you? To act justly and to love mercy and to walk humbly with
your God."

—Micah 6:8

Why

The wasteland of "why" boils with a lonely, dark heat.
It blisters against the tender pieces of my heart—the core of
my soul;
I brace; the storming blast of difficulty will take its tortured
toll.
The putrid smell of this barren land fills my senses.
And like water circling down the drain, I will lose all of my
best defenses.
On bended knee I beg before the throne of grace;
I crawl with weary frame with dusty ground upon my face.
In whispered words against my tears I plead for desert mercy.
Still, the wasteland's bare way stretches in miles and miles
before me.
"WHY" . . . my heart longs to understand.
It is the question my mind rolls over and repeats time and
time again.
How could this wasteland pass to me through Your loving
hand?
"WHY" does faith take seed in soil that's fertilized with pain?

In tender voice, I hear You say, *"My child, you must follow me.*
It's not for you to question the plans you cannot see.
Now put one foot in front of the other, and walk in wasteland heat.
And, when passing through the suffering 'WHY,' you'll be behind
my feet.

You walk no place I have not stepped; this trial is not for loss.
Your heart's deepest questioning leads to the ground beneath the cross.

You ask me 'WHY' still, and still I ask you to obey.
Dear one, listen to My words and keep in step with Me today."

"Let us fix our eyes on Jesus, the author and perfecter of our faith, who for the joy set before him endured the cross, scorning its shame, and sat down at the right hand of the throne of God. Consider him who endured such opposition from sinful men, so that you will not grow weary and lose heart."

—Hebrews 12:2–3

Big God

God is big enough for all my questions
And for my toughest thoughts.
He understands my feelings
And all my flaws and faults.

God is big enough for all my questions
And for my hardest fight.
He understands my fear
And what keeps me up at night.

God is big enough for all my questions
And for pain I cannot comprehend.
He understands my weakness
And what yields my knees to bend.

God is big enough for all my questions
And for each time my heart asks "Why?"
He understands my journey
And what prompts my heart to cry.

God is big enough for all my questions
And for all my problems too.
He understands ME . . .
And what my feet will step through.

"But the Lord is the true God; he is the living God, the eternal King. . . ."

—Jeremiah 10:10

Light

Orb of cloudy, washy-white,
Perpetually charged,
Shines into the ethereal dark
And needs no further instruction
To be a faithful night light.
Glowing, simply because God spoke . . .

"And God said, 'Let there be light,' and there was light."

—Genesis 1:3

He Loves Me

I stand before the throne
of the One whom I have known
since the warm, spring day
when I gave my rags away
for a new life!

"Therefore, if anyone is in Christ, he is a new creation; the old has gone,
the new has come!"

—2 Corinthians 5:17

He Is the Light

He is the Light that pierced the darkness,
    Amid the stormy sea.

He is the Light that pierced my darkness,
    The light that came for me.

He is the Light—resplendent bright,
    The Bright Morning Star!

He is the Light—brilliant bright,
    Who will find you, wherever you are.

". . . 'I am the light of the world. Whoever follows me will never walk in darkness, but will have the light of life.'"

—John 8:12

Abide

Seasons pass,
The story hides,
The scar fades.
Hours fall into days,
God abides.
But trouble still finds me,
Which is *why* I must abide!

"I am the vine; you are the branches. If a man remains in me and I in
him, he will bear much fruit; apart from me you can do nothing."

—John 15:5

For the Display of His Splendor

Bloom

THE DAY LILIES IN MY garden are blooming. They are take-your-breath-away beautiful with their delicate features and palette of colors. The petals appear as velvet in the early morning sun and serve as a changing canvas throughout the day. Their individual colors intensify with the absorption of light. God, the Creator and the Gardener, displays His glory.

My garden is a mixture of plants and perhaps a good representation of my life. Amid day lilies and roses, small yellow squash are beginning to appear, and the crabgrass covers one corner of a bed. Water bowls for dogs sit underneath every outdoor faucet, along with countless tennis balls and half-chewed items that have long passed recognition. It is not a place of perfection; however, it is a genuine place. Life is real in the garden—real weeds, real bugs, real dirt and sweat, real peace, and real beauty.

The day lilies are my favorite. They captivate me and move

me to gratitude, as all but a handful were gifts from people who love me. The lilies are the heart of my hodge-podge garden displaying a splendor of beauty that reminds me that God's compassions are new every morning.

> *"Because of the Lord's great love we are not consumed,*
> *for his compassions never fail. They are new every morning;*
> *great is your faithfulness."*
> —Lamentations 3:22–23

I was not born with a green thumb, which may explain my tolerance for the crabgrass. The same friends who graced me with dozens of lilies once bought me a garden plaque that read, "I tried, but it died!" My sister's contagious love for gardening, and my heart's desire to spend time with her, inspired me to begin following her to the lily fields. These delicate flowers inspired me with a passion for gardening while stirring scripture in my heart. How could I have ever known all the words God would speak over my heart through my garden? My sister once said, "I love lilies because they will grow anywhere for anyone." Indeed, they are hearty. Day lilies will bloom despite their circumstances, in often unfavorable situations, among the debris of real life, simply because the Creator says, "Bloom."

As I walk in the garden, my heart focuses on the words of

Jesus found in the Gospel of Matthew: "See how the lilies of the field grow. They do not labor or spin. Yet I tell you that not even Solomon in all his splendor was dressed like one of these" (6:28–29). Is it no wonder that Jesus compares our freedom from the entanglement of worrying to the course of a lily's beauty? After all, we are God's creation.

Throughout His ministry, Jesus called people to set aside worry and anxiety. He taught and demonstrated that circumstances do not author our lives. He alone is the Creator, the Author of Life, and the Provider of all our needs. In the message of Matthew 6, Jesus is inviting the people to trust Him. He is challenging them to live a life abandoned to loving God and seeking God's will for their life apart from the stress and entanglement of worldly concerns. Jesus never said the world was free of debris—real troubles, real fear, and real pain; however, He boldly proclaimed that He had overcome the world.

> "... *In this world you will have trouble. But take heart!*
> *I have overcome the world."*
>
> —John 16:33

Jesus transcends our current situation and imputes His peace and joy amid the trials of everyday life. Just as God

formed Adam in the dust of the garden and brought forth his life, God brings forth life today in the real circumstances of our everyday lives.

In the dust of my garden, God is capable and willing to provide for all my needs. How beautiful our faith must appear before Him when our hearts yield to worship and our lives bloom with perseverance regardless of the debris, simply because the Creator says, "Bloom."

"Consider it a sheer gift, friends, when tests and challenges come at you from all sides. You know that under pressure, your faith-life is forced into the open and shows its true colors."

James 1:2–3 (The Message)

Our lives have the opportunity to be take-your-breath-away beautiful before the Creator.

Vessels

The potter's hands skillfully wrought
A vessel designed with loving thought,
For purposes greater than temporal gain,
Crafted with hands that divinely ordain
Each moment, each eyelash, each detail measured;
A beloved water pot—adored and treasured;
The basin's beauty reflected in souls that taste
The Living Water of God, flowing forth in grace.

*"Whoever believes in me, as the Scripture has said, streams of living water
will flow from within him."*

—John 7:38

I Wonder; I Remember

When my heart gets overwhelmed and busy,
My calendar full of appointments like an overstuffed
mix of laundry,
I wonder: am I missing time with just You and me?

When I read through scripture and fail to notice the
words,
My study homework completed but not really filled in,
I wonder if I've got the point of studying completely
backwards?

When my prayer life is filled with love notes, but not
love,
My heart, mind, and soul distracted and focused
elsewhere,
I wonder what deep conversations with You I'm falling
short of?

When my concern or kindness becomes about an inch
deep,
My actions toward others more about me than You,
I wonder if I make You look superficial and cheap?

When I'm just a wreck, a wretch, a complete mess,
My life full of fumbled moments and way too many
feelings,
I wonder if You still love me? And then I remember—
On my worst day, *You gave me Your Best.*

*"But God demonstrates his own love for us in this: While we were still
sinners, Christ died for us."*

—Romans 5:8

All

Lord, I want to love You, and not the idea of loving You . . .
I want to hear Your words in quiet moments and
piercing sound.
I want to laugh with You over the silliest of things,
recognizing Your chuckle.
I want to keep my feet behind Yours and step on
hallowed ground.

Lord, I want to love You, and not the idea of loving You . . .
I want to hear the song You sing over me while I sleep.
I want to wake up in the morning and see the sunrise
You painted.
I want to experience You fully . . . as deep calls to deep.

Lord, I want to love You, and not the idea of loving You . . .
I want to dig in the garden with You and soak up the
miracle of creation.
I want to see You in the tiniest details of my day.
I want to flee from immorality and avoid temptation.

Lord, I want to love You, and not the idea of loving You . . .
I want my words to be filled with humility, forgiveness,
and grace.
I want to see my neighbors the way You see them.
I want the seat of my heart to be Your special place.

Lord, I want to love You, and not the idea of loving You . . .
I want my heart, my mind, and my soul to do a cartwheel
by Your side.
I want to give You my feelings, my thoughts, and my
attitude.
Lord, I want to love You as much on the inside as it looks
like I do on the outside!

Lord, You want me to love You, and not the idea of loving You . . .

*"'Teacher, which is the greatest commandment in the Law?'
Jesus replied: 'Love the Lord your God with all you heart and with all
your soul and with all your mind.'"*
—Matthew 22:36–37

Have a Cup of Coffee

Have you ever desired the emotional forecast
Of the busy day ahead?
Have you ever hit your snooze button
And crawled back into bed?

Have you ever counted every penny
And wondered where they went?
Have you ever stared into your mirror
And frowned with discontent?

Have you ever forgotten the milk or the meeting
And burnt the breakfast toast?
Have you ever compared dirty dishes to dirty laundry
And wondered which one you despised the most?

Have you ever counted calories or fractions
Prior to consuming a therapeutic level of caffeine?
Have you ever pitched your tent in a rut
And walked the treadmill of routine?

Have you ever felt like you tossed life's instructions away
Because they simply seemed too complex?
Have you ever lost your temper, your keys, or your patience
And pondered if your mind was next?

Life can be hectic.
Slow down, pour a second cup of coffee this morning,
Talk to God about your thoughts,
And read His Word.

"Blessed is the man who does not walk in the counsel of the wicked or stand in the way of sinners or sit in the seat of mockers. But his delight is in the law of the Lord, and on his law he meditates day and night. He is like a tree planted by streams of water, which yields its fruit in season and whose leaf does not wither. Whatever he does prospers."

—Psalm 1:1–3

Clang

How do I sound in Heaven?
When I hold the door for someone but evaluate their
clothing. *I think I must clang. . . .*
When I let someone have the better parking place but I
envy the car they drive. *I think I must clang. . . .*
When I deliver a meal to someone in need but
complain about the inconvenience. *I think I must
clang. . . .*
When I loan a possession to my neighbor but count the
debt against them. *I think I must clang. . . .*
When my lips offer forgiveness but my heart still holds
the grudge. *I think I must clang. . . .*
When I volunteer my time for a project, but I seethe in
silent resentment. *I think I must clang. . . .*
When I greet others with kind words but engage in
gossip. *I think I must clang. . . .*
How do I sound in Heaven,
When the music of my life plays before the throne?
I desire to sound like the sweetest music—perfect pitch,
perfect tone.
But I think I must clang when I love others less
And serve them from a heart that is *only serving* to
impress.

"If I speak in the tongues of men and of angels, but have not love, I am only a resounding gong or a clanging cymbal."

—1 Corinthians 13:1

Page 1880

Held steadfast in the wind, joy abiding
Through the storm's deep wake,
The tormentor's worst chiding.
Grief renders despair the heart alone knows;
Melody of character suffering can transpose.
Trials render beauty, that others might see
The nature of Jesus revealed through me.

"Consider it pure joy, my brothers, whenever you face trials of many kinds, because you know that the testing of your faith develops perseverance. Perseverance must finish its work so that you may be mature and complete, not lacking anything."

—James 1:2–4

Heart Prayer

Father . . .
Teach me to love others as You do,
Let Your peace flow through my life,
Clothe me in deep joy, abiding,
Anoint my heart with patience,
Adorn my lips with Your kindness,
Plant Your Word in my heart,
Guide my feet to follow Your steps.

"I pray also that the eyes of your heart may be enlightened in order that you may know the hope to which he has called you, the riches of his glorious inheritance in the saints, and his incomparably great power for us who believe. That power is like the working of his mighty strength."

—Ephesians 1:18–19

Pictures to Take

Sunlight touches my window,
My toes touch the bedroom floor.
Anticipation of unfolded lilies
Is the lone alarm clock I adore.
Capturing the lily's peaceful beauty—
an aide memoir that God walks with me.
Morning sun's kiss is my choice make-up.
Talking to Him, grabbing my camera,
Taking the time to fill my coffee cup,
I quietly find my way out the back door.

"Give ear to my words, O Lord, consider my sighing. Listen to my cry for help, my King and my God, for to you I pray. In the morning, O Lord, you hear my voice; in the morning I lay my requests before you and wait in expectation."

—Psalm 5:1–3

Thanksgiving

I worship before the King,
Knowing nothing I gain or bring,
No riches or talent I possess,
No acquisition of knowledge I learn
Could purchase my forgiveness
Or secure the grace I could never earn.
I came to His throne in brokenness,
In poverty of spirit; now, I yearn
To know the One whose name I bless,
Who gave His life for my life's mess.
Jesus is my heart's true thanksgiving.

"O Lord, open my lips, and my mouth will declare your praise. You do not delight in sacrifice, or I would bring it; you do not take pleasure in burnt offerings. The sacrifices of God are a broken spirit; a broken and contrite heart, O God, you will not despise."

—Psalm 51:15–17

Sandpaper

Like sandpaper,
The word *suffering* scrapes my throat.
I long for it to roll like honey from my tongue,
But, that hasn't happened yet,
And the likelihood that it will seems remote.
I am surrounded by reminders
That Jesus stands firm in the storm,
And I am held firmly in the storm,
So why do stormy winds cover my eyes with blinders?
Why do trials still stump my toes?
Why can't my transformed heart be fully reposed?
In the chaos of the dark night, Jesus is near,
So why does my heart kick up doubt and fear?
Why am I so slow to understand
the lesson of suffering passing through God's hand?
Tell me, why do I allow my courage to slip,
Silencing the song of joy passing through my lips?

"I love the Lord, for he heard my voice; he heard my cry for mercy.
Because he turned his ear to me, I will call on him as long as I live."

—Psalm 116:1–2

The Truth Isn't Always Pretty

Be still!
I can hardly count to ten
Without wondering again
If I should stop and count to ten!

Be still!
I run around like mad all day
And don't have the time to hear You say,
Be still, sit down, listen, and pray!

Be still!
I move from one busy thing to another.
I don't have the time; I don't make the time
To stop and think of others.

Be still!
Lord, if You want to see fast-paced—my life is it,
And, You want me to sit?
You've got to be kidding me?

Be still!
Chores keep me busy until I collapse each night,
And You want me to sit
And make the time to be quiet?

Be still!
I have a growing list of things I really need to do;
Lord, I simply don't have and can't make
The time to be with You.

How did I get so busy? So crammed with activity?
And when did my life become all about me?
Why do I struggle to juggle it all?
How did my schedule make God useless and small?
Why did I litter my calendar with appointments?
Why is my organization so stressful and tense?
And why can't I slow down and be still during my day?
At one point, did I start following God this way?
In the skewed perception of busy life, I realize that I have
failed to see
That by refusing to be still, I have asked the Lord to follow
me!

"Be still, and know that I am God; I will be exalted among the nations, I
will be exalted in the earth."

—Psalm 46:10

Grace Today

My broken heart left to bear
Will often wonder why life isn't fair,
And trying moments in season's pressing
Will persuade my thoughts and leave me guessing.

IS GOD'S GRACE ENOUGH?

As seasons pass as waves on sand,
The Lord teaches my heart to understand
The truth that rings resplendently clear:
His grace is greater than my deepest fear,

His grace is sweeter than each lonely day,
His grace speaks over what others say,
His grace is sufficient; His grace is *ENOUGH*;
My heart's work is to simply give Him all my stuff!

So, on winter days, when bitter air
Chaps my face without concern or care
And draws the sadness from my face,
I'll lean into God's ample grace.

On summer days, when sticky air
Blows storming winds that make others stare
And draws the shame from my face,
I'll rest in the sweetness of sufficient grace.

Through the days of fall, when lukewarm air
Feeds passing time that whitens my hair
And draws the youth from my face,
I'll draw my beauty from God's beloved grace.

And on spring days, when near-perfect air
Wisps through my smile with loving flair
And draws the joy from my face,
I'll lift my voice to sing of God's amazing grace.

As days into the seasons pass,
When crowded thoughts with feelings amass,
I want my heart to reflect, my life to say,
God's Grace is enough for me today!

"But he said to me, 'My grace is sufficient for you, for my power is made perfect in weakness.' Therefore I will boast all the more gladly about my weaknesses, so that Christ's power may rest on me."
—2 Corinthians 12:9

Prayer from My Heart

Dear Abba Father,
When my feelings, my words failed to portray,
I found You leaning closer to me.
As moments defied understanding,
You spoke truth over and into my soul.
When the path beneath my feet left me with no words to
say,
You helped me find my voice and allowed me to see
That when I am broken, my faith is made whole.
The story I narrate
Is of Your tenderness and compassion,
Your strength and peace blended with grace.
Truly, when I felt as though I was being crushed,
Abba Father, You lifted and carried the weight.
Your love is beyond what I could imagine.
In trials, the voice of faith is never meant to be hushed.
The song of Your joy lifts from such a place.
So, when my words fail me yet again,
My prayer will be to sing.

"But let all who take refuge in you be glad; let them ever sing for joy. Spread your protection over them, that those who love your name may rejoice in you. For surely, O Lord, you bless the righteous; you surround them with your favor as with a shield."

—Psalm 5:11–12

The Path Beneath
My Feet

Sandy Sandals

ONE OF THE MANY THINGS that I enjoy about being a woman is the opportunity to follow Jesus in a variety of shoes! I can follow His footsteps in heels, clogs, house slippers, or cowboy boots. In truth, each style and pair of shoes that graces my feet is a pair of shoes designed for following. In my everyday routine, whether I'm in flip-flops at the grocery store or tennis shoes on the treadmill, I am a follower of Jesus. My shoes, my wardrobe, my surroundings, and my circumstances may all change, but my heart and my feet should remain steadfast behind the feet of Jesus.

Living in the Deep South, where it can feel like summer ten months of the year, I have the luxury of wearing sandals year-round. And, as much as I *adore* a great pair of high heels, sandals adorn my feet more than any other style of shoe.

As I completed the last treatments of chemotherapy, I found myself longing to sit on the beach. I wanted to feel the salty air in my hair and on my skin. I wanted to soak up some vitamin D, and I wanted to look across the ocean and know that my Savior walks on top of the waves. For many reasons that are complex and personal, I both *wanted and needed* to follow Jesus to the beach. Consequently, I spent many days on the beach with my family that summer. Somewhere along the path of that blessed journey, I began taking photographs of both my feet and my sandals. And it was in taking those photographs that I came to a deeper understanding of following and a deeper, precious understanding of His blessings along the path. The captured image of my *sandy sandals* serves to remind me that *I am to follow.*

I am to follow Jesus in fair weather and storms. I am to follow when I am rested and when I am fatigued. I am to follow in places both beautiful and lovely and likewise in places that are possibly horrific and soaked in stench. I am to follow in my office, in my kitchen, in my garden, and in my grocery store. I am to follow in all circumstances.

There have been times when I failed to see the path God placed beneath my feet, and there have been times when fear got the best of me and I stopped walking. It can be complicated to trust God with perfect timing in my life. It can be fearful to follow His footsteps when I cannot see the plans and steps ahead. In my times of limited sight and in my times of faltering, God remained faithful. I have come to understand that He will part the ocean floor, if

needed, to create a path beneath my feet. He is not limited by circumstances, and the word *obstacle* does not exist in His vocabulary. He is the *best, most precious Father*.

Following Him with a heart of devotion calls for application of His Word. If I know the Word of God but fail in application, I will falter in following. The application of God's written Word in my life changes my heart. And my feet, adorned in a variety of shoes, will follow the love of my heart—my Jesus.

The poem "Time" was written during the early days of my battle with breast cancer. It serves as a reminder that whatever circumstances I face, God is ever good and faithful. I can trust Him, and I can put my hope in Him.

My prayer is to keep my feet solidly behind His; I want my sandals to be filled with the sand He kicks up as He walks.

Purpose

Lord, how could I have seen the path
You placed beneath my feet?
Lord, how could I have known the people
You expected me to meet?

Lord, how could I have measured the seeds
You purposed my life to sow?
Lord, how could I have comprehended
The path You requested me to follow?

Lord, Your eyesight is unhindered and unlimited,
You see the sand in the deepest abyss of the sea.
Lord, You abide even when I failed to understand
That path You drew and blessed for me.

~

*The first stepping stones of this path were laid in the devotion of
my heart.*

~

*"'For I know the plans I have for you,' declares the Lord, 'plans to prosper
you and not to harm you, plans to give you hope and a future. Then you
will call upon me and come and pray to me, and I will listen to you. You
will seek me and find me when you seek me with all your heart.'"*

—Jeremiah 29:11–13

Blinded

Despair and fear, wasteland heat

Amalgamating a pasty covering,

Affecting my eyes to fail to see

The path God placed beneath my feet.

*". . . And I pray that you, being rooted and established in love,
may have power, together with all the saints, to grasp how wide and long
and high and deep is the love of Christ, and to know this love
that surpasses knowledge—that you may be filled to the measure of all
the fullness of God."*

—Ephesians 3:17–19

My Steps

The order of the steps is not mine to complete.
Even in this darkness, the somber hour's tint
Can never change the love of God
Or for whom His grace was meant.
In the wrenching journey's moments,
My Father has a parent grip on me.
Within His hand, peace and calm
Will stand against the churning sea.
And He will part the ocean's floor,
If needed, to create a path beneath my feet.

"I know, O Lord, that a man's life is not his own; it is not for man to direct his steps."

—Jeremiah 10:23

Follow

Too precious to put into words, too sweet to fully explain
The day He found me—the moment He spoke my name.

My heart did a cartwheel; my mouth filled with song
The day He loved me—and I knew He had loved me all
along.

For the first time, I could breathe; the haunting darkness
departed
The day He claimed me as treasure—my abundant life
started.

Too wonderful to keep to myself; I long to share the story,
The day He paid my debt in full—exchanged my filth for
His glory.

How resounding the joy, how deep a love I would know
The day Jesus called my name—inviting me to follow.

*"'Come, follow me,' Jesus said, 'and I will make you fishers of men.' At
once they left their nets and followed him."*

—Matthew 4:19–20

Divine Artist

If I drew my life in doodles
And painted each day in hues,
The dark pigment of the storm
I most likely would not choose.

I'd be terribly tempted to draw
A butterfly life, painted in with pastel.
I would doodle the rosy path and
Ignore the shallow life story I might tell.

Thankfully, my hands don't hold the pen,
The marker, the brush, or the adze,
And I don't pick the tools and colors
That shape and paint my days.

It is not my place to direct my steps;
That task belongs to the One
Who gave His life to redeem my life—
God's One and Only Son.

With joy, and in surrendered heart,
I choose to give those tools away;
The Carpenter, the Painter, Jesus the Creator
Is the divine Artist of each of my days.

"I am the Alpha and the Omega, the First and the Last, the Beginning and the End."

—Revelation 22:13

Found

It was so dark . . . so very dark.
I remember wondering if light could touch darkness.
I felt exhausted—I felt worthless—I felt hopeless.
Grime covered me . . . I was shadowed in guilt.
My sense of self lived in a glass house that I had built.

I was so broken . . . so very broken.
I must have looked like the mess I felt like, the day He
found me.
But He never saw anything but my worth and my beauty.
Jesus came for me—Jesus died for me—Jesus became my
sin.
Light pierced the darkness . . . and I was born again.

I was transformed . . . completely new.
Jesus was enough—Jesus is enough—Jesus will be enough,
amen.
I will never be lost in the darkness again.
I am loved—I am treasure—I am a child of the King.
Salvation planted a song in my heart that I continue to sing.

*"For God so loved the world that he gave his one and only Son, that
whoever believes in him shall not perish but have eternal life."*

—John 3:16

Grace Insight

Lord,
I am halted and I am humbled
by the grace given to me from Your hand.
I did not earn it, nor deserve it,
and when I rubbed Your face
in the moments of my worst day,
when I came desperate and broken,
dirty from living in the vomit of life,
You forgave me
and welcomed me to abide in You.

"... *Blessed are they whose transgressions are forgiven,*
whose sins are covered. Blessed is the man whose sin the Lord will never
count against him."

—Romans 4:7–8

The Garden Path

The garden path captivates me
And bids me wake to walk with Thee,
To see the treasure bright and new
Nestled fresh in morning's dew.

The pebbled path beneath my feet
Imbues my day with grace so sweet;
The flooding fragrance of morning's light
Speaks to Your watch kept through the night.

The robin's song a background pleasure
Against the brilliance of garden treasure,
Flowers displaying to fill an outdoor vase,
And amid their beauty, I seek Your face.

No better place have I found to see
The vast expanse of Your love for me
Than on the path Your garden keeps;
I follow in love behind Your feet.

"On my bed I remember you; I think of you through the watches of the night. Because you are my help, I sing in the shadow of your wings. My soul clings to you; your right hand upholds me."

—Psalm 63:6–8

Time

This day has passed with urgency.
Still, I felt as though it lasted a long time.
Just last week, I cut my hair with the carefree attitude of
summer.
Just last week, I was carefree?
I have yet to spend a lazy, hot day on the beach;
Even my shoulders are missing the sun-kissed tan of June.
A flat of annuals sits, waiting to be planted in my garden.
I thought I had time . . .
Now I sit waiting.
I find myself mentally rearranging my schedule.
Lying on tables, I consider that it's time for peaches to ripen.
I remember I had planned to make jam this year.
And now I need to choose a surgeon.
Lying in a machine, I force myself to focus on anything else.
My thoughts land on time with my children.
And, although I try very hard not too, I wonder
how much time . . .
The sand falling through my personal hourglass has been
sifted.
Internally I scream, "I'm quite certain I don't have time for
all of this . . ."
Wait, I'm not sure I was asked that question!

Lucid, I realize the tumors growing in my chest demand my time,
And they did not need my permission to give me this day.

"We wait in hope for the Lord; he is our help and our shield. In him our hearts rejoice, for we trust in his holy name. May your unfailing love rest upon us, O Lord, even as we put our hope in you."

—Psalm 33:20–22

My Gardener

John 15 Thoughts

E VERY BIBLE I OWN CONTAINS notes, bookmarks, or scraps of paper marking the fifteenth chapter of John's Gospel. I don't know how to completely explain the words God has written over my heart in the garden, nor do I know how to describe the vast fullness of His presence that I experience when I'm in the garden. All I know is that *He is my Gardener—the Vinedresser of my life.* My southern tongue would describe Him as the *Farmer of my days.* Regardless of the circumstances that surround me, the words of John 15 touch a chord in my heart—that special place where only God's hand reaches. I followed God into the garden, and it was as though I discovered a whole universe of His magnificence. His vast, personal love for me became infinitely apparent, and I am forever changed.

The *Gardener* captivates me. As I was working to finish this book, these words left my pen one afternoon:

Working in the garden,
I hear the music the seasons keep.
Buds morph into blooms,
Grass keeps rhythm and grows tall once again.
Lawnmowers buzz and hum,
Weeds join the al fresco choir.
Afternoon thunderstorms—booming and bringing
Cymbals to the sky, with quiet wonder.
Bright sunshine fills every room,
Both inside and out.
Likewise, I smile,
Smelling of dirt,
Sneezing from pollen;
I pull the weeds this afternoon
Listening to the sound
Of
Spring singing
Winter to sleep.

The specific words reflect my experience in the garden, but they could have just as easily been about any other afternoon subject. Growing in my relationship with God, I have come to understand that my circumstances and/or surroundings do not alter God's abiding. They do not alter His truth. They do not alter His caring. He is a *hands-on Gardener!*

If we have weeds of doubt or fear growing in our life, God sees. If the soil of our heart needs nurturing, God nurtures. If we are broken-hearted, God mends. If we are in pain, God comforts. If we are hot, thirsty, tired, needy, discouraged, or bored—God knows.

In the garden dirt, in the hammock, in the hospital waiting room, God always abides with us. And when we abide in Him, then He makes each of us like a well-watered garden.

"I will always show you where to go. I'll give you a full life in the emptiest of places—firm muscles, strong bones. You'll be like a well-watered garden, a gurgling spring that never runs dry."
—Isaiah 58:11 (The Message)

Lily Beds

Alone here with the Gardener,
In the lily bed, I never pretend.
Rather, I see myself reflected
    in the dirt of the garden.
My stained hands find flowers to attend
As I give over the concerns
God's peace alone transcends.
Gardening to a song selected
To express my gratitude for this place,
Where He walks with me.

"I am the true vine, and my Father is the gardener."

—John 15:1

184

First Frost

Bright, bright sunshine falls across my garden,
Cool, crispy air stings my cheeks,
Scattered blooms tell of summer's bounty,
Pine needles decorate every outdoor container,
My dog's light coat is changing into thick fur.
She and I both seek the sunny spot in the yard for a nap;
I soak up the last warmth of this day, knowing
tonight the first frost will tuck my flowers into bed.
Fall brings a rest to my garden
Until the cool, smooth air of spring blows off the winter
blankets.

"Your love, O Lord, reaches to the heavens, your faithfulness to the skies. Your righteousness is like the mighty mountains, your justice like the great deep. O Lord, you preserve both man and beast. How priceless is your unfailing love! Both high and low among men find refuge in the shadow of your wings."

—Psalm 36:5–7

Day Dream

I would love to garden beside the Lord
And see how He stakes His tomato plants.
We would laugh and sweat together,
And I could ask Him about the purpose of fire ants!
We could pitch pine straw around the flower beds,
While the morning shade hung over our heads.
And I would love to see His hands dig for sweet potatoes
And hear His comments on the wandering, wild rose.
We could pick peppers and peas and persimmons together.
I could look at the sky, speculating on tomorrow's weather.
(I'm guessing He would chuckle at that notion!)
He and I could catch a farmer's tan under the southern sun;
We would discuss how many zucchini one tiny plant can
yield!
And we could eat fresh watermelon in the field;
Laughing, we would allow the sticky juice to run down our
chins.
And both of us, no doubt, would find our summer grins,
With purple fingers and mouths full of fresh-picked
blueberries!

If given the chance to garden beside the Lord,
He and I would plant and prune on hands and knees,
Until we collapsed together in a bed of lilies.

This was my dream today, while I gardened on my knees,
Transplanting flowers and reclining in the grass,
And my heart was filled to the measure
At the thought that one day, *this day dream* might come to
pass.
Oh, how I hope to garden in Heaven, beside the Gardener.
He is my Lord—my love and my treasure!

*"Who has measured the waters in the hollow of his hand, or with the
breadth of his hand marked off the heavens? Who has held the dust of
the earth in a basket, or weighed the mountains on the scales and the
hills in a balance?"*

—Isaiah 40:12

Claws, Please!

Perched on ankles impersonating stools,
Working in the garden, I pause.
A little green lizard stands not more than two feet
Away from my seat.
Aware that he can leap farther than that,
I whistle for my cat,
Who happily lends me her claws—
The preeminent gardening tools!

"As water reflects a face, so a man's heart reflects the man."

—Proverbs 27:19

Camellia Queen

Storm-weathered, deep-rooted,
Abounding in garden soil that is suited
For her every need,
The camellia perches over the new bed
With blooms like eyes of pink and red,
Keeping watch over fresh seed.
A thousand petals flaunt her blush,
Her beauty causing the flora youth to hush.
Unquestioned is her splendor.

*"Therefore, as God's chosen people, holy and dearly loved, clothe your-
selves with compassion, kindness, humility, gentleness and patience."*

—Colossians 3:12

Lily Thoughts

Unveiled wonder,
Dancing color
Catching the light,
Teasing my eyes,
Bearing fruit,
Displaying craftsmanship,
Decorating my life;
How grateful I am
To witness this beauty,
The lily's loveliness
Lifted from the Creator's hand.

"Do everything without complaining or arguing, so that you may become blameless and pure, children of God without fault in a crooked and depraved generation, in which you shine like stars in the universe as you hold out the word of life."

—Philippians 2:14–16a

Winter Flora

Transverse across an oak leaf-laden patch;
Her petal-heavy arms are no match
For summer's bounty heat,
So she'll litter her beauty,
Greeting the warmth once more,
With her adornment lying at her feet
Like jewelry discarded upon the floor.

"Do you not know? Have you not heard? The Lord is the everlasting God, the Creator of the ends of the earth. He will not grow tired or weary, and his understanding no one can fathom."

—Isaiah 40:28

This Counselor's Couch

Flip-flops, potting soil,
A flat of spring annuals,
Curls set in ponytail mode,
Shovel and spade in my hand—
Much-loved Garden therapy.

"O Lord, you are my God; I will exalt you and praise your name, for in
perfect faithfulness you have done marvelous things,
things planned long ago."

—Isaiah 25:1

Who?

Who knew
Day lily dew
Dripped like velvet rain?
Who knew
Day lily dew
Could speak to my pain?

This morning,
A drop lands on my toe,
And I know
That God knew
The power of day lily dew!

He is, after all, the Gardener of my life!

"By wisdom the Lord laid the earth's foundations, by understanding he set the heavens in place; by his knowledge the deeps were divided, and the clouds let drop the dew."

—Proverbs 3:19–20

Maiden

Replacing mulch, browned from wintry fade,
I catch the perfume of spring,
Refreshing and new,
The clement sun escorting her down the aisle
With all the loveliness of a June bride's maid.

*"From the fullness of his grace we have received one blessing
after another. For the law was given through Moses; grace and truth came
through Jesus Christ."*

—John 1:16-17

Mary Van's Garden

The garden I see is created with loving mentation,
   A peaceful place where beauty blooms.
   Faithfulness built this al fresco room;
  Rich, velvet petals sunbathe in the heat of day,
  Hinting at God's immeasurable imagination.
My eyes are captured, my breath taken away
As I behold the color of long-suffering love,
Stained in the palm of my sister's garden glove.
I am drawn to the quietness that exists here
   —Serenity encircling elation—
In this beautiful garden, God is near,
And I am walking in His creation.

"In the beginning God created the heavens and the earth."

—Genesis 1:1

Mary's Easter Morning

Walking early, in the garden mourning,
Seeking her Lord in moments weighed
With heart of grief and emotions frayed,
Distraught beyond the comfort of men,
She's lost her Lord, her dearest friend.
She longs to know where He's been taken,
When in her heart a new song awakens.

Jesus said to her, *"Mary."*

She failed to know His voice—His face,
But her spoken name all doubts erase.
Jesus stands before her—the Risen Lord;
Her sorrow gives way to joy restored.
Jesus speaks with her; He loves her so.
Her moment of truth is the truth I know;
Mary bears witness to Easter morning.

"Jesus said to her, 'Mary.'"

—John 20:16a

"The watchman opens the gate for him, and the sheep listen to his voice.
He calls his own sheep by name and leads them out."

—John 10:3

He Sees Me

Blurry Feet

THE FOLLOWING STORY WAS WRITTEN in my journal, and it has served as a challenge for me to remember that God sees me. He is watching.

In the hundreds of pictures I have snapped beside the wrestling mat, most of my favorites are not in complete focus. Quite often I capture two blurry images on the bottom of my son, Jeff's, legs—his feet. I know this seems strange, but in my amateur understanding, Jeff's blurry feet generally imply he's winning!

Of course, I love to photograph his face. And, occasionally, I luck up and get a great shot of his jaw line—firmly locked. John and I have learned to recognize the locked-jaw determination that settles around his boyish face during a match. When Jeff sets his jaw line and starts moving those big feet, he's coming hard at his opponent. He's wrestling to win!

The most cherished photographs include both his face (in determined focus) and his feet (nothing but a blur . . .).

When wrestling first became a part of our life, I knew

absolutely nothing about the sport. I spent the entire first season trying my best to discern whether Jeff was winning or losing on the mat. When he had wrestled his last match that year, I had learned two clear facts about the sport.

First, if you pin your opponent, you win.

And, second, you can't win the match if you keep your head in the mat.

GET YOUR HEAD OUT OF THE MAT was the one phrase that every other mother in the gym seemed to understand and use with both frequency and volume. It was well into the second season before I understood the significance.

In wrestling, when your head is down and your face is shoved into the mat, it is almost impossible to find leverage. And, leverage is necessary to stand over your opponent.

The one who stands or prevails is the victor.

The apostle Paul understood the concepts of wrestling, and he had a working knowledge of leverage. In his letters, he frequently urges and instructs believers to stand firm in their faith and in the strength of the Lord.

In Ephesians 6:10–13, Paul writes these words of instruction to all believers: "Finally, be strong in the Lord and in his mighty power. Put on the full armor of God so that you can take your stand against the devil's schemes. For our struggle is not against flesh and blood, but against the

rulers, against the authorities, against the powers of this dark world and against the spiritual forces of evil in the heavenly realms. Therefore put on the full armor of God, so that when the day of evil comes, you may be able to stand your ground, and after you have done everything, to stand."

So often in our daily walk with the Lord, we struggle to stand. If the bold apostle were in our presence today, teaching this message, I think he would look around our world—our cubicles, our neighborhoods, our living rooms, our schools—and shout, "GET YOUR HEAD OUT OF THE MAT!"

In our daily Christian walk, we can be guilty of functioning in a defeated, head-down position. Symbolically speaking, we live with our head pressed into the mat. In ordinary situations, we settle for feeling trapped, overwhelmed, and weighed down. Instead of leaning into the Lord, we lean into our own understanding of circumstances, which leads to discouragement and confusion. Scripture is very clear: the wicked schemes of the evil one are prevalent, and they are specifically designed to leave us feeling defeated. Trusting in our own strength leads to reckless and ineffective behavior.

If Satan can keep our face pressed into the mat, he has the advantage. However, Paul's carefully chosen words for power or strength unveil this truth: when we are strong in the Lord, we have an unmatchable advantage because we have unmatchable leverage.

We have the Lord's leverage; we have His strength, His power, and His might.

As dearly loved children of God, we were not meant to walk around in despair, fear, or defeat.

We were God-designed, with locked-jaw-determination, to be victorious. We were created to stand.

In the remaining verses of Ephesians 6, Paul gives a detailed description of the armor of God. His words are unmistakably clear: putting on the armor of God equips us to stand.

If God was photographing you on the wrestling mat of your day, would He get a great shot of your beautiful, blurry feet?

My Psalm 18 Moment

The putrid smell of the storm fills my nostrils.
I struggle to concentrate.
I feel battered.
The water has raged against me . . . wave upon wave upon
wave.
I feel small.
My energy and courage would not fill a thimble.
I feel weary.

I think to myself, "This is what it feels like to emotionally
drown."

And then I see Him.
He's walking toward me,
His feet gloriously positioned on top of the waves.
He smiles at me and calls my name.
He reaches down and scoops me out of the water.
His powerful arms wrap around me.
He draws me close to His chest.
He smells wonderful!
I breathe in the deep aroma of love.
My Jesus is Lord over the storm.

"He reached down from on high and took hold of me; he drew me out of deep waters. He rescued me from my powerful enemy, from my foes, who were too strong for me. They confronted me in the day of my disaster, but the Lord was my support. He brought me out into a spacious place; he rescued me because he delighted in me."

—Psalm 18:16–19

Treasure Surrendered

In the garden, alone with God,
I found my voice.

Chaotic noise had overtaken the quiet.
And it was a simple choice
To be silent before Him.
In the quiet, by the Gardener's side,
The lily's beauty touched me
In a way I've yet to fully understand.

My heart was lead to surrender
—Completely surrender—
The treasure I held so tightly in my hand.

Words were found as fractured tears fell
Upon the petals I prefer.

My faith—like the tall pine tree,
Quietly grows.

~

*Lord, open the fingers of my clenched heart, and lead me to let go;
sustain me in moments when I am tempted to pick up what can
only abide in Your hands.*

~

"*Because of the Lord's great love we are not consumed, for his compassions never fail. They are new every morning; great is your faithfulness.*"

—Lamentations 3:22–23

Good Day

The smell of fresh dirt in my hair at night
Likely means winter's polish has faded from my fingernails.
I dig the dirt to relieve stress,
And I plant to see God bring new life from soil.
I marvel at the colors of the Creator's creation,
I pray the words of David's psalms.
Playfully, I splash the top of my toes with bright colors,
I navigate life in flip-flops,
I rake pine straw and nap in the hammock,
And I sing to the chat-chat-chat of the lawn sprinkler.
As spring's heat awakens my summer heart,
I fall asleep to the cricket's courting song.

"Those who are wise will shine like the brightness of the heavens, and those who lead many to righteousness, like the stars for ever and ever."

—Daniel 12:3

Tears

The rain falls quietly,
Landing on my eyelashes momentarily.
It trickles down my cheeks,
Following the course my tears trace,
Finding its way into the palm of my hand
As I wipe its path from my face.
If only my tears were erased so effortlessly.
The rain falls quietly, as I cry.

"The Lord is close to the brokenhearted and saves those who are crushed in spirit. A righteous man may have many troubles, but the Lord delivers him from them all."

—Psalm 34:18–19

Savannah's June

Warm air encircles me.
The summer light of June is fading.
The lilies have closed business for the day,
While the morning glories steadily work
to swathe the thick pine trees.
My cat's deep purring vibrates against my feet.
Traces of potting soil hide under my fingernails.
Contentment sits among my thoughts.
Still and quiet before the Creator,
Listening to the southern insect melody,
I let the hammock swing me to sleep
As the silver slipper of the moon
hangs in the evening sky.

"For I am convinced that neither death nor life, neither angels nor demons, neither the present nor the future, nor any powers, neither height nor depth, nor anything else in all creation, will be able to separate us from the love of God that is in Christ Jesus our Lord."

—Romans 8:38–39

I Am Loved

I am plastered with His love,
I am covered with His grace,
I am held close to His heart,
I am held close to His face.

I am carried in His arms,
I am protected by His power,
I am sheltered by His peace,
I am sheltered this very hour.

I am filled with His joy,
I am comforted by His hand,
I am encouraged by His Word,
I am encouraged where I stand.

I am immersed in His friendship,
I am overflowing with His blessing,
I am strengthened by His strength,
I am strengthened by the King.

"God is our refuge and strength, an ever-present help in trouble."

—Psalm 46:1

Tame the Tongue

I can get really tripped and snared
When all my dirty laundry's aired.
As gossip blows in the wind,
I find I must be disciplined
To ignore the words that cut my skin
And forgive from my heart time and again.
My selfish self will put a locking grip
On steps that cause my feet to slip.
When others seem to burst my bubble,
My words can stir the pot of trouble.
When circumstances blow apart,
I've been known to argue with my heart
On the slippery slope that leads to *me*.
Using language both biting and nasty,
I have reached for words piled up inside,
When clearly spewed, quickly hide,
The Lord's reflection . . .
OUCH! . . . my hasty words should heed inspection!

Sometimes it's best to remain quiet,
Even when I think I'm right.
Speaking wisely, I protect my walk
By closing my mouth to malicious talk;
Giving my mind time to breathe

Will slow my words before they leave.
God alone can tame my speech
When in yielded heart, I let Him teach.
My days are blessed when my tongue is lead
By the thoughts He captures, the words left unsaid.

"Do not let any unwholesome talk come out of your mouths, but only what is helpful for building others up according to their needs, that it may benefit those who listen."

—Ephesians 4:29

Tossed Down Truth

Lord,
Called to toss upon the sea,
Raging
Water over my head,
Blinding,
Flooding through my heart—
I wonder how and why this happens.
Treading water,
I falter.
I long for the deep rest of a thousand days,
A time of springtime across my path.
I wonder,
Can the seasons change upon this ocean?
I pray.
Lord, can You call forth rest upon these waves?
Gulping water,
My heart shriveled as my hands,
I tread the turning water,
Realizing
That You swim next to me!
That You swim for me!
My struggling efforts to escape the storm,
To find You elsewhere,
Are foiled.

Abba Father, You are walking here.
And my heart, so full of pain,
My mind confused,
Knows and accepts
That treading water in this storm
Is my only place of rest.
In the churning water,
You teach my heart to swim,
Gulping a mouthful of truth.
Upon the puke of this tossing sea,
I am called and loved,
And I follow You.

*"The man who loves his life will lose it, while the man who hates his life
in this world will keep it for eternal life. Whoever serves me must follow
me; and where I am, my servant also will be. . . ."*

—John 12:25–26

Seen

Lord, Your words and Your kindness
Speak to the wounds of my affliction,
To the developed leprosy of my heart.
In this trial's wake, You see my distress.

"I waited patiently for the LORD; he turned to me and heard my cry.
He lifted me out of the slimy pit, out of the mud and mire; he set my feet
on a rock and gave me a firm place to stand. He put a new song in my
mouth, and hymn of praise to our God. Many will see and fear and put
their trust in the LORD."

—Psalm 40:1-3

Reading Your Word

Lord,
Time and time again, I come to this place;
I long for the refreshment of calm and quiet,
When You touch the tears that stain my face
And speak to the thoughts that stalk my night.
Lord, create in me a new heart—fully dedicated.
Brush away the worry that encircles my throat,
Equip my feet to follow the path before me unabated,
As my fingers unfold pages, touching the story You wrote.

"Sanctify them by the truth; your word is truth."

—John 17:17

Acknowledgements

Fʀᴏᴍ ᴍʏ ʜᴇᴀʀᴛ, I ᴀᴍ thankful to my husband, John, for helping make this book a reality. He lovingly tolerates my disorganization and works beside me with anticipation even as I litter our home office with notes, notes, and more notes. He sacrificed so that I could rest, and recover, and write; his friendship and love ever-blesses me.

I am grateful to Stephen and Marianne for their openhanded gift of allowing me to dig and transplant hundreds of day lilies from their garden.

I am grateful to my sister and brother-in-law, Wendy and Richard, for their hospitality, inspiration, patience, and generosity. Many of the photographs included were taken in their day lily garden, *Mary Van's*, located on Cowart Farm, in Bloomingdale, GA.

With respect, I am grateful to those who invited me to listen and trusted me with their story.

I am grateful to the wonderful women who have studied the Bible with me. Their walking beside me --their friendship-- has been a paramount piece of this book.

Lastly, I would like to thank my children, Erin, Wesley, and Jeff They have been supportive along each step of this journey, and demonstrated patient understanding through the long hours of typing, reading, and organizing. It is my joy to be their mother, and I love them every day, deep in my heart, all the time.

For more information about
Jo Crosby
&

Wherein the Lilies Grow
please visit:

www.priorityinsight.com
jo@priorityinsight.com
www.facebook.com/priorityinsight

....

For more information about
AMBASSADOR INTERNATIONAL
please visit:

www.ambassador-international.com
@AmbassadorIntl
www.facebook.com/AmbassadorIntl